BEYOND
ACCESSIBILITY

BEYOND
ACCESSIBILITY

Toward Full Inclusion of People with Disabilities in Faith Communities

Brett Webb-Mitchell

Church Publishing
NEW YORK

Unless otherwise noted, the Scripture quotations contained herein are from the New Revised Standard Version Bible, copyright © 1989 by the Division of Christian Education of the National Council of Churches of Christ in the U.S.A. Used by permission. All rights reserved.

Cover design by Christina Moore/Laurie Klein Westhafer
Typeset by Beth Oberholtzer

Library of Congress Cataloging-in-Publication Data

Webb-Mitchell, Brett.
    Beyond accessibility : toward full inclusion of people with disabilities in faith communities / Brett Webb-Mitchell.
       p.   cm.
    Includes bibliographical references.
    ISBN 978-0-89869-641-7 (pbk.)
    1. Church work with people with disabilities. I. Title.
BV4460.W4275   2010
261.8'321–dc22

                            2010000023

Church Publishing, Incorporated.
445 Fifth Avenue
New York, New York 10016

www.churchpublishing.org

5 4 3 2 1

To the people in all faith communities
who share a vision of the Church as the fully inclusive body of Christ,
a place and people for and of all God's people.

CONTENTS

ACKNOWLEDGMENTS

This book came about many years after I wrote *Dancing with Disabilities*. I thought I had written my last book or paper on people with disabilities with that book. Then a few years ago, the Rev. Peter Sulyok, then the director of the Advisory Committee on Social Witness Policy (ACSWP) of the Presbyterian Church (USA) asked me to be the writer of, and a consultant on, a project to formulate a new policy for the denomination on issues facing people with disabilities in the Church and world. Sitting with my friend the Rev. Dr. Trace Haythorn over breakfast at one of the Committee meetings, Peter challenged the members of the Committee to write a policy that would be the last one that needed to be written because full inclusion of people with disabilities would be the goal, and after full inclusion, what else would there be to do? Not only that, this paper was to be a social witness policy not only to the Church, but to the world. Believing that life is a process, a journey, a pilgrimage, I understand now that while the paper I worked on for and with the Presbyterian Church (USA) was a "next step" toward advocating accessibility and acceptance of people with disabilities in the Church, the paper fell short of mapping a way forward toward full inclusion.

This book hopefully challenges the reader and the Church toward considering the next step, the next move, in the Church's pilgrimage toward being and becoming fully inclusive of *all* people who are called and desire to be part of a faith community. *Beyond Accessibility* is a book that challenges and celebrates the many ways that faith communities are or are becoming more totally inclusive of *all* God's people.

I want to thank all the individual people and faith communities whose stories are in this book, making it almost a book of narratives rather than a theological text. Many thanks to Rich Dethmers of Henderson, North Carolina, whose story opens this book poignantly and honestly. I met Rich when I was interim pastor of First Presbyterian Church, Henderson, NC when Elder Phil Hanny and I went to visit a "shut-in." What blossomed was a friendship that eclipsed a pastor to shut-in relationship. I am also honored by all of the people who shared their stories and lives unaware that I was listening and watching at the time, from my time in the L'Arche Lambeth community in the West Norwood section of London, England, to the people who attend the various churches where I have been an interim pastor during the last few years.

Thanks to those who gave me a running start at this book who were part of the ACSWP Committee called to write the new policy paper on people with disabilities in the Church. I especially want to thank Peter Sulyok and Trace Haythorn for their trust in me as writer and a consultant in that noble project. I hope this book more or less captures what we talked about on the fringes of our Committee's meetings over three years.

To those who helped bring my scattered thoughts and ideas into cogent theological and biblical propositions, especially Sr. Stef Weisgram of St. Benedict's Monastery in St. Joseph, Minnesota, Dennis Ford who read this book line by line, and Ryan Masteller who carefully managed me and this book into production.

I want to thank senior editor Frank Tedeschi for his ongoing belief in my work, studies, and ideas. In a world of "publish or perish" from which I came from as an academician, Frank has kept me "alive" in many ways. His constant support has given me the encouragement I needed in writing the next book after each book I've published with Church Publishing.

Finally, to my family, I owe a great debt of gratitude as I spent countless hours writing and thinking of the ideas that are somewhere in this text. To Dean my partner and to Parker and Adrianne my children: many thanks for pushing and prodding me to not only write but practice inclusion in my daily pilgrimage of life.

PART ONE

Images for an Inclusiveness Community

So we, who are many,
are one body in Christ,
and individually we are members
one of another. —ROM. 12:5

I n reading and rereading the Apostle Paul's letters, covering primarily the very complex, mystical, just-beyond-reach feeling of being the body of Christ, one of the grammatical points made by Paul about the body is that he is not explaining the Church *as* the body of Christ by using a metaphor or analogy. Paul isn't talking about "the Church" being *like* a body or *as* a body. For Paul, the Church *is* the body of Christ.

Saying that the Church is the body of Christ makes a difference in how we perceive or comprehend who and whose we are as members of the Church, regardless of whether modern society labels us "disabled" or "able-bodied." What does Paul's charge and blessing for us to be the body of Christ mean in our individual parishes and congregations generally? For our family? For our neighborhood? For the world around us? More specifically, what does it mean for a church today in terms of moving beyond accessibility for people with disabilities when we reflect the peculiarities of this body, "in which God arranged the members in the body, each one of them, as he chose . . . where there may be no dissension within the body, but the members may have the same care for one another" (1 Cor. 12:18, 25)? For if we asked or surveyed most Christian communities, "Does this reflect your congregation or parish in regards to people with disabilities?" my hunch is that the answer would be (honestly) "No."

In part one of this book, we explore the nature of the body of Christ as it pertains to the act of welcoming, accepting, and including the fullest participation of people with disabilities, recognizing that all of us—able-bodied and disabled alike—have gifts, talents, and services. Again, as I read, reread, hear, preach, and teach on this subject, I am convinced that Paul is saying something dramatically different about the communal nature of the body of Christ than what many churches understand "being church" with one another means. I have come to this conviction in large part because of my experience worshipping with so many communities of faith with people with disabilities.

Part one is divided into four chapters. The first chapter is a "State of the Church" address, outlining where we've been, are, and are going. The second chapter surveys the nature of what *is* the body of Christ. In particular, I am interested in the kind of membership there is in the body—women and men, Jew and Greek—and discovering what we can learn about the head of the body itself, which is Christ.

The third chapter focuses on the gifts, talents, and services that are integral to the body. The key to this chapter is Paul's conviction that membership in the body of Christ does not require a certain social adaptation score, an intellectual quotient, a particular social class, or any of the other artificial criteria that may be prized highly in today's Church. I will return to this point frequently in the pages that follow. The fourth chapter focuses on the dynamics of the relationships that we have with each other within the body. In particular, I want to focus on those passages where Paul distinguishes the "less honorable" and "more respectable" members of the body of Christ. I've been with many groups of people with disabilities, including their advocates and guardians, who are quick to point out that these distinctions include or pertain particularly to people with disabilities, especially when they are judged as being "inferior" with a disability in today's world.

Collectively, the four chapters of part one provide an argument for the full inclusion and participation of *all* members of the body of Christ, the Church. After all, the only thing that matters in being a member of the body of Christ is that we are "activated by one and the same Spirit, who allots to each one individually just as the Spirit chooses" (1 Cor. 12:11).

CHAPTER ONE

Introduction:
Beyond Accessibility

"People react weird to people with disabilities like me," said Rich, sitting comfortably in his modern electric wheelchair. "They act like a disability is something they can catch, like it is infectious. At church, most people are unable to get past my disability. They stare not at me but at my disability." I sit in the taupe Lazy Boy recliner directly across from him. While I am not sure if I can separate a disability from someone's personhood—anymore than I can separate gender, race, or sexual orientation from someone's personhood—I think I get the point: people look at his wheelchair and his body sitting in the chair—with a brace supporting his head, and the limp position of his left arm, hand, and legs—rather than at him. From time to time during our conversation he casually moves one of his two fingers on his right hand onto the space-age control pad situated on the right armrest to adjust and readjust the wheelchair to a height and reclined position that is comfortable for him.

From where I sit in his family's large, austere living room, furniture pushed aside to make it easier for Rich to move around in his wheelchair, I silently admire his chair and the technology behind and in it. His chair is incredibly sophisticated in all its electronic marvels; even the ergonomics are intriguing to my naïve eyes. While I study and admire the chair in the comforts of his living room, I quickly remember a time in my life when wheelchairs were not so sophisticated.

At the time, I was working in my first position as a music therapist at a state hospital for children and adults with multiple physical, emotional, and developmental disabilities. I would push children in larger-than-life metal wheelchairs, that were universal in size and not made to fit any human body per se, through cheerless, cluttered hallways of a state institution—called a hospital back then—for people with developmental disabilities or, as it was called then, "the mentally retarded." Not surprisingly, the generic wheelchairs often did not accommodate the small bodies of the children. In response, carpenters on the grounds made some rather crude physical adaptations to the basic wheelchairs without changing the chairs themselves. The challenge for the carpenters was to craft chairs for children of all shapes, sizes, and disabilities. For example, carpenters added a fascinating array of cushions and pads to fit the shape and requirements of children with microcephalis (unusually small head and underdeveloped brain), hydrocephalis (unusually large heads because of the build up of fluid inside the skull, leading to brain swelling), and sometimes for young people with almost paralyzing cerebral palsy, seizure disorders, or other physical disabilities. The strategy for building a customized wheel chair usually involved taking a basic wheelchair—it seemed that all that was available in those days were big, medium, and small sizes—adding a pad to separate the legs so that they wouldn't rub together, and then attaching a large "S" shaped pad in the back to protect the patient from further scoliosis or curvature of the spine. At the top of the chair the carpenters usually affixed two large padded mounds that looked like lollipops on a stick, making it possible for a person to be angled in such a way that their head would fall backwards onto the blue plastic-covered cushion rather than falling forward. Automobile seat belts were attached to the metal frame to keep the child in the chair. There were no electric chairs at the institution. An electric wheelchair like the one Rich sits in today was, at that time, a dream for the future, a la "Star Trek."

The future is today.

I've been to Rich's Dutch Colonial style house several times over the year because he is a member of the church where I am interim pastor. He is also one of the "shut ins," a category given to those people who are not able to leave their homes easily. Usually this category means those who are elderly and infirm. In this case, Rich is not elderly (he is my age, after all, and I'm not elderly), but he is infirm. Rich has made it to worship only once in the last year since I've been interim pastor—Christmas Eve to be exact—so, along with another Elder of the church, I bring Holy Communion to his home from time to time. My bringing him the elements of Holy Communion at home is easier for him and his family. Since Rich has become more limited in the use of his limbs because of his multiple sclerosis (MS), it often takes a great deal of effort to get Rich out of the house and into the church. Such an adventure—even though the church building is only a few blocks or roughly a half-mile from the home—takes Rich and his family some time to get him dressed, get him into the van, get him out of the van, get him into the church, and get him down the aisle to the place where there is a half-pew space for wheelchairs.

So I bring Communion to Rich, and in our time together I realize the truth behind Jesus' promise: wherever two or three are gathered in my name, I am there (Matthew 18:20). The Spirit of Christ is in our discussions about life, God, and the Church, and in sharing Holy Communion with one another.

Our discussions of topics related to the Church in particular, and Christian life in general, are not a stretch for Rich. Rich is a "P.K.," an abbreviation for what we in the church business translate as a "Preacher's Kid." Rich grew up in New Jersey, raised in a home where his dad was a minister in the Reformed Church of America and his mom was the minister's wife and a nurse. His mom, now deceased, was initially annoyed that Rich hadn't asked Jesus to heal him. Rich tells me that he did ask to be healed but, well, sometimes for no rhyme or reason these things just happen in life.

Today, Rich is married and is a proud father of three strong-willed, creative children, and grandfather of three. Rich had a successful career as a hospital administrator for most of his life, having worked at the nearby community hospital before multiple sclerosis[1] progressed to such a point that it now controls most of his body.

Rich's perspective on living with a disability is not sugarcoated or draped in a romantic, faithful banter that minimizes the pain of living with a chronic disease and physical disability. The challenge may be compounded by living in a small Southern hamlet, in which people with certain disabilities, especially those in motorized wheelchairs, are still a rare sight, unlike larger cities, where people in motorized wheel-chairs blend into the fabric of the urban environment. Multiple sclerosis is no joy ride. "Shit happens," he has said more than once. In less than twenty years he has gone from being a healthy young man to being almost bedridden, save for the hours he spends in his wheelchair, with the only voluntary movements left in his body being in his right arm and two fingers, along with his ability to talk. He has a lively imagination and is incredibly smart. When I ask him what it is like to live with multiple sclerosis, he takes a deep breath, waits a beat, and tells me, "Eighteen years ago or so I was chatting with a small group of people about how I was doing living with MS and I related that I had some foot drop, fatigue, and had to stay out of the sun or symptoms exacerbated but otherwise not too bad. An older man in the group who had mild MS but both his wife and daughter had more severe MS said to me, 'It's going to be a tough life,' and he was right." The upside of living with multiple sclerosis, if there is one? "Learning patience."

Rich is a man of faith. And that faith is genuine and sincere. I sensed that from our conversation in his home when we first met a few months ago. He is somewhat angry at God for allowing multiple sclerosis to come into his life, but he is also thankful for the good support of his family, including brothers, sisters, parents, kids, wife, and others. Although he came to church twice a month when he was able to get around on his scooter, his time of going to church has been limited by the progressive nature of his degenerating neurological condition. He can do less and less by himself, and more and more of his everyday life requirements are placed on the other members of his family. Because it is now physically daunting to get into the sanctuary, even though there is an elevator and the church's front pews have been cut to make it possible for him to "blend" into the congregation—though his big black chair sticks out amid the white pews with red cushions—he has stopped coming to worship because it is too much of a physical challenge to simply get there. He keeps up with church activities through paper newsletters, computerized messages, and visits from the pastor. In addition, he deepens his theological interests by reading books with a spiritual message.

Before I left his house one day, I asked Rich when he met God at the proverbial Pearly Gates, would he be in a wheelchair or walking. "Walking," he said without missing a beat. "When I dream at night I am walking. I am never in a wheelchair in my dreams. I won't be in a wheelchair when I meet God either."

Crossroad: Between the Past and the Future

I begin this book with Rich's story because he embodies the latest crossroad we find ourselves at in this journey of faith communities and the "community" of people with disabilities.[2] The path we choose at this juncture will determine and shape how people with disabilities will discover their place, role, and function—or in theological language their gifts, talents, and services—toward the greater good of all of us who are members of the Church, the body of Christ.

The Church must choose either to go forward in faith, stay right where it is, or—worse yet—go back to where it once was. In the past we, the Church of people who are burdened with hidden disabilities or non-disabled, have been in relationship with or treated people with visible disabilities largely as objects of charity. As objects of charity, the view is often taken that an impairment has been foisted upon a person from birth because of a birth "defect" such as Down syndrome, or due to one's age like Parkinson's disease that usually strikes people over the age of 40, or are victims of their own disability-marred future, like someone who contracts cancer from smoking or is HIV positive. There are still people in this world who believe a child's disability is somehow or the other related to the sin of a parent or forbear.

Now, with large brush strokes and broad generalizations, here is the ongoing dilemma: regardless of how one contracted the disability, condition, or limitation, the Church views and hears that person as "handicapped" and as someone to be pitied, rather than as a human being who lives with a limitation or disability. Charity is foisted upon the individual, whether the individual has asked for it or not. Or, alternatively, the person with a disability becomes merely a teaching tool for pastoral care types who want to help the rest of us who are non-disabled to discover our mortal limitations or the vacuous nature of our rat-race lives.

Sadly, many people with disabilities did and do not know that there was an option, a choice, for doing or being something different than simply being a case study or object of charity. While those with physical or sensory disabilities—being blind or deaf for example, or those who live with allergic reactions to certain perfumes, scents, gluten, or peanuts—knew and know that they have a choice or option for how they will be perceived in the world, many people with intellectual or social disabilities were not always aware or know they have an option of how they wanted to be known and related to by others. The lack of role models who did not "fit" society's image of being "disabled," the failure to be with others with intellectual or social disabilities in learning how to reshape the public's viewpoint or perspective, left many to be shaped by the un-informed public. People with intellectual or social disabilities were and are often simply disempowered or disenfranchised by the majority of people who are non-disabled.

More recently, out of a mixture of guilt and the "Golden Rule," otherwise known in Church circles as Jesus' command for us to "do unto others what we would want them to do to us" (Luke 6:31), some people who are non-disabled in congregations and parishes have "made it possible" for or "allowed" more people with disabilities to be part of a church by making a limited number of physical and programmatic accommodations. For example, consider Sunday school programs just for people with certain intellectual disabilities, and perhaps a special worship opportunity outside the normal worship service on Sunday morning for the same people. The words in quotation marks above dramatize the inequality of power, within which people who are non-disabled have the sole power to determine how a church structure or program will be made accessible for people with disabilities. For example, Rich openly acknowledges that the Church building is physically or architecturally accessible to a person with physical disabilities, though he is reluctant to say how accessible it might be to someone with a *different* kind of disability, like an intellectual disability.

Though this will be discussed later in this Introduction, the reason that many of our church structures built prior to the 1960s were not accommodating to people with disabilities is because the majority of people with disabilities were simply not present. People with disabilities were not living by themselves in houses or apartments, in group homes (there were none to speak of), or with their families, and thus were not in our communities or neighborhoods. Many people with disabilities were living in institutions for people with disabilities, with one of the oldest institutions reaching back to the sixteenth century, with the creation of "St. Mary of Bethlehem Hospital for the Insane" in London, England. And before that, many people with disabilities of all kinds were left to fend for themselves in the alley ways, by ways, and sitting by the city gates or pools of healing, much of which reaches back to biblical times, as recounted in various Gospel stories (Luke 14:15–24, John 5:1–15). In response to this lack of entry into the hearts, minds, and houses of worship, there was a grassroots movement in the 1960s to form intentional communities of people who are able-bodied and disabled. The goal of these faith communities like L'Arche Lambeth was the full inclusion of people with disabilities in every aspect of the life of the community; indeed, the presence of people with disabilities was the raison d'être for the community itself. The problem for many intentional faith communities that include people with disabilities is that often the people with disabilities did and do not have a choice as to whether they want to be part of these communities. This infuriates many people with disabilities who, in more recent days, are part of a self-advocacy or self-determining movement, whose goal is to assure that everyone with a disability exercises their right to choose where they live, work, worship, play, vote, and learn. Many people in the self-advocacy movement believe that, without this choice, those living with disabilities in such intentional communities are kept more or less dis-abled—literally not able to speak or communicate for themselves—and thus disenfranchised.

So this thumbnail sketch shows us where we are at this juncture of the road, with a decision to be made as we *both*, the Church and people with disabilities alike, try to figure out which path we are going down from here. Do we maintain the status quo by offering limited physical and programmatic accessibility for the few who can be assisted by family advocates and friends? Or do we, the Church, follow the lead of the majority of people with disabilities—and their family and friends—who rightfully and faithfully want us *all* to move forward. Do we need to treat people with disabilities not as charity cases or as second class citizens (and this is being polite) but as full citizens within the body of Christ that is the Church. Do we, the Church, engage and work with people with disabilities in making sure that everyone is provided opportunities to discover and use their God-given gifts, services, and talents through full participation and leadership in the body of Christ? And furthermore, do we, the Church, move forward by working with people with disabilities toward the full recognition that we are *all* created in the image of God and are members of Christ's body, even moving beyond modern society's perception that divides the world into a duality of the "disabled" and "able-bodied"?

In other words, how would the Church look, sound, feel, and move as a fully inclusive body of Christ? More to the point: how would a church feel or be if a person's abilities or disabilities really didn't matter at all? After all, our place in the body of Christ is not predicated upon what one can or cannot do, but upon who and whose we are: God's.

In order to better understand the groundbreaking challenge of being the inclusive body of Christ, let me quickly suggest that there are three "phases" that society has gone through in terms of positioning people with disabilities in relationship to society as a whole, and the Church in particular. First, recognizing that the past is prologue for the present, I briefly examine the period of segregation and seclusion, in which people with disabilities were neither seen nor heard. Second is a period of mainstreaming, when the special education class model used in the public schools was adopted by the Church. In this second phase, people with disabilities were brought together in one space, but set apart in that one space, modifying the "separate but equal" situation in most educational classrooms and worship spaces or sanctuaries. The third and most recent period is represented by the self-determination movement toward genuine inclusion. People with disabilities of all kinds are no longer waiting for permission to join a church. They roll into worship, use sign language during times of fellowship, participate in service projects by any means possible, seek to be leaders and pursue ordination as ministers, priests, or pastors, being unapologetic about asking for and using different modes of communication to take classes, pass ordination exams, and minister to the larger church.

Segregation and Seclusion: Neither Seen nor Heard

I was recently on Ellis Island, touring the many hallways of the vast main building, and was searching for the area that addressed the way those who were immigrants to this new land were treated upon landing on the Island. The historians who put together the exhibits remind us that people with any viral contagion were quickly quarantined to another building on the vast campus. Those who struggled and lived with what we call today intellectual, social, or behavioral disabilities were some of the first people to be subjected to a battery of tests that would later become known as IQ or intelligence quotient tests. For example, nine out of one hundred people were marked with an "X" for additional mental examination, and out of those nine, one or two were held for further inspection. In the early part of the twentieth century, researchers like Henry Andrew Knox and Henry Herbert Goddard first used tests that looked at people's ability to perform simple intellectual functions—like math and geometric puzzles—to see if people were "mentally retarded." The fear was that people with developmental dis-abilities—which were apparently deemed "not good" and unaccept-able—were being brought into the United States through Ellis Island. Goddard brought the Binet-Simon Intelligence Test from France, using this simple performance test—putting objects in order according to height, counting, and other manipulation of objects—to quantify peo-ple's intelligence. Persons who scored lower than the average or mean were deemed "mentally retarded." This test was the prototype for the latest test of intelligence, the Stanford–Binet test, which many of us have taken in public schools to measure our IQ. Of course, many times the greatest barrier for being successfully tested was simply language, as most of the examiners only understood English, and most of those tested did not understand English.

In the last century in the United States, people with disabilities—physical, visual, hearing, intellectual, and mental illness—were com-monly placed in institutions that were located far from centers of population. The image of such institutional life was captured in the important book by Burton Blatt, *Christmas in Purgatory*, a collection of photos from an institution in New York revealing the decrepit nature of institutional care in the 1940s, 1950s, and early 1960s. I worked in a somewhat better venue in my first institution—the Delaware Hospi-tal for the Mentally Retarded that was formerly called the Stockley Colony for the Feeble Minded—that was located outside of George-town, Delaware, in the middle of corn and soy fields and chicken coops, far from Wilmington, Dover or Salisbury, Maryland. At first, the argument was made that these institutions were created to provide care for people with disabilities that they would not otherwise get from their families of origin or the public at large. As cited above, people with disabilities would often have to fend for themselves any way pos-sible, given that there were no societal programs for those who were impaired, poor, hungry, without shelter, or desolate. Later, the argu-ment changed. People with disabilities were institutionalized not only for their education and well-being, but also for the well-being of the family of origin. In other words, people with disabilities were separated from the life of the family of origin and became, to both the family and society at large, out of sight and out of range of being heard.

These institutions were meant to provide people with disabilities all that they would ever need in life, from education in the early years to work on assembly lines performing simple tasks such as putting nuts and bolts together. Food and healthcare, rudimentary education, shelter, clothes, and religious services were provided by and within the institution. Needless to say, those who were institutionalized were rarely if ever seen in a community or neighborhood community of faith. Only those with hearing and/or visual disabilities, along with those who were ageing but whose intellectual abilities were never compromised, were welcomed to sanctuaries of faith. There were day trips for the institutionalized, but they were rare. For those who became pregnant, forced abortion and sterilization was handled quietly, and often on the institution's grounds. Only a few years ago, the state government of North Carolina apologized to the individuals who were sterilized in institutions against their will. To this day, many of the institutions that opened at the turn of the last century still host cemeteries with the records of those who died while institutionalized lost or misplaced, leaving us to wonder who has been buried in those hallowed grounds. This is the case of St. Elizabeth, in the Washington, DC, area, where the records of who is buried where have been lost in the dust of history.

Mainstream: In the Same Room, Yet Separate but Equal . . . Sort Of

In the 1960s, the social civil rights movements that affected the place and presence of African Americans, farm workers, women, and lesbians and gays, also included people with disabilities. Through the work of parents with children with intellectual disabilities, the Association of Retarded Citizens or ARC, came into being as parents increasingly demanded that their children with disabilities have a proper education. This movement received the support of the late President Kennedy and the Kennedy family, especially Eunice Kennedy Shriver and the creation of the Special Olympics, and Jean Kennedy Smith and the creation of the Very Special Arts movement.

"Deinstitutionalization" brought many people with disabilities out of the institutions where they once lived, either entering the public square for the first time in their lives and fending for themselves, or placing people with disabilities with their family of origin, extended family, friends, advocates, or group homes spread throughout our communities and neighborhoods, whether we live in the city, the suburbs, or the rural back roads. Quite quickly, faith communities were and are struggling with the place and presence of people with disabilities in their midst. The sudden outpouring of so many people with disabilities into communities and neighborhoods caught many people flat-footed in making a response to the sudden presence of people with disabilities in the public square, including faith communities. There were few health service professionals who were capable of working with community groups in preparation for the inclusion of people with disabilities. Some communities of faith rose to the challenge and learned to worship, be in fellowship with, and embrace the new members who happened to be disabled, while most other churches shunned people with disabilities and their families, indicating to the person with a disability that she or he was not welcome.

Here's an indicator of how swift the change was in our churches' response to the presence of people with disabilities in our midst: in the 1950s and early 1960s, no churches had "handicap parking" spots with the omnipresent and ubiquitous blue sign with the white stick figure in the wheelchair. Now, many churches not only have parking spots for people with disabilities, some use this very same logo on their websites, bulletins, and newsletters to show that their church is welcoming of people with disabilities. I know of families with children with disabilities—from Down syndrome to youngsters with Attention Deficit Hyperactivity Disorder or to those in a wheelchair—who were searching, entering, and joining (when possible) churches. They brought their children up front for children's sermons before young ministers who did not know what to do with these children who were sometimes more outspoken than other children seated around the person giving the message. I have heard many stories of families with children with disabilities, who were asked to leave the church because a child was "uncontrollable," talking loudly or strolling up and down the aisle during worship. And there are stories of religious leaders leaving faith communities because they could not work or worship with people with disabilities. Ramps to doorways–usually the front door–of faith communities were quickly constructed, with or without approval of town councils and historic preservation councils. Many doorways were poorly thought out, as the doors often swung toward the person in the wheelchair, who was trying to get in, rather than moving laterally with the push of a button or swinging away automatically from the person approaching in a wheelchair. Those who had ageing children, adult siblings, spouses, or partners in significant long-term relationships with disabilities came to church in hopes of finding a community resource that would offer aid and sanctuary for their family members when the non-disabled sibling, parent, partner or guardian died.

Beginning in 1978, people with disabilities–classified as one of the largest, if not *the* largest minority group in the US–were on the move to expand their access to education, housing, and civil rights. The passage of three pieces of legislation was especially significant. Public Law 94-152 assured education for *all* children regardless of abilities or disabilities; the Fair Housing Act (504) secured the rights of people with disabilities to own homes; and the Americans with Disabilities Act (ADA) in 1990 expanded the civil rights of people with disabilities. People with disabilities were not waiting politely and patiently for their family and friends to bring them to a faith community anymore: they were and are either coming or not coming of their own volition.

Meanwhile, some churches continue to maintain their ramps and electric doors, making a bathroom here or there easy to enter. Others have chosen the mainstream or "separate but equal" approach to living with people with disabilities. In special education, the mainstream approach meant putting a student with a disability–whether it be an intellectual, developmental, behavioral, social, or other kind of disability–into a regular age and grade-appropriate classroom setting for most activities. However, this approach nevertheless continued to remove the child with disabilities to another classroom or a separate area of the classroom for other activities, such as the study of math, science, English, and history. Following the models established by educational institutions, mainline denominations created programs for a specific audience of people with disabilities–in effect sequestering them from the rest of a group for special instruction in the same classroom space–instead of examining the larger questions that define discipleship, nurture, praxis, or catechism in the life of a church. Many churches still provide a "best buddy" program, linking a person with a disability to a non-disabled person, with usually the person who is non-disabled making the choice of who the "best buddy" will be. I still receive email messages about a separate (but equally meaningful) Monday evening worship service in my home town of Chapel Hill, North Carolina that is offered to people with intellectual or developmental disabilities as an alternative to the Sunday morning service. Similarly, separate fellowship opportunities for *only* people with intellectual and developmental disabilities still sprout up from time to time.

The state of the Church today seems to be as follows: on the one hand, because there are no governmental laws that force the hand of a community of faith to shape or make changes in their structures or programs, many churches still either exclude people with disabilities by sins of "omission"—not having any accessibility into a church because they had not thought of it—or by sins of "commission" when they voluntarily choose not to welcome people with disabilities. On the other hand, many churches who are trying to be more inclusive are caught between the models of segregation and mainstreaming. Some churches provide little more than a parking space for a person with a disability, while others offer a few opportunities for some, but not all, people with disabilities. So while the rest of modern society races to be more inclusive of people with disabilities, the Church has continued to drag its heels in becoming a fully inclusive community of faith. Many churches have made their buildings more accessible but then have failed to look at the next step, the next issue: full inclusion of all who wish to worship, pray, serve, teach, learn, be in fellowship, and lead the people of God, regardless of what they choose or can or cannot do. Sadly, for most churches, the status quo, the duality of "us versus them" between people with disabilities and people who are not disabled, remains.

Toward Full Inclusion: Of and With People with Disabilities

The subtitle of this book "Toward full inclusion of people with disabilities in faith communities" is the primary theme of this book because it is the next step, phase, or move that needs to be made to go beyond welcoming and merely accepting that a person with a disability is present among congregants and parishioners. The Church body is challenged to move over, adapt, re-think, re-imagine, and re-consider what is the "norm" for worship, prayer, fellowship, education, and service, and make a place for and with those who are part of one of the world's largest "minority groups." In recent years pressure for inclusion has come from the community of people with disabilities—whether they are located in towns large or small, urban or rural—who have become and are media savvy, politically active, and culturally significant. Even the categorization or label of what is a "disability" is being strongly challenged. For example, some people with a hearing impairment or disability are now deconstructing stereotypes and labels by redefining themselves as a culture unto themselves. In addition, self-advocacy and self-determination as the next new "wave" in the disability rights movement means that simply adding ramps outside of our faith community's buildings or a special education Sunday school curriculum is no longer adequate or even acceptable.

Simply put: people with disabilities are demanding full and total inclusion within communities of faith and the public square. It is a matter of justice. It is a matter of love.

So what does "inclusion" mean? The Latin root of the word "inclusion" is roughly translated to "to shut in" or "enclose." In other words, people with disabilities are asking if not demanding for the equal right to be included and thus "shut in" or be "enclosed" within faith communities of their choice, like the rest of us who self-identify as "nondisabled" are within communities of faith.

But there is something more going on here. It means that to be included or enclosed is also to exchange the verbiage of "*those* people with disabilities" or "them" versus "us," for the language of "we-ness" or "ours" within and among members of faith communities.[3] What people with disabilities are asking for is what people who are non-disabled are asking for in parishes and churches: that the gifts, services, and talents in each of us, as persons created in the image of God and saved by God's grace, be identified and used for nurturing the common good of all in the body of Christ. In other words, the push is to go beyond simply being "there" in communities of faith to full participation and leadership, depending upon the gifts and services, talents and loves, of the person with a disability. In this, people with disabilities demand nothing more and nothing less than to be like any other member of a church or parish.

Here's another way of understanding inclusion. In the 1980s, "inclusion" and "inclusivity" became the "catchwords" of the education strategy of special educators and social activists in the "disability"[4] community. For example, instead of placing a child or young adult in a standard classroom for part or the entire day, with the expectation that the student would keep up with the work, inclusion involved rearranging not only the classroom's physical layout, but the entire curricula and class of students as well. The ideal is this: a classroom that is inclusive will serve a cluster of people with and without disabilities, not just a single person. The goal? To see that people with disabilities and those without disabilities will not only see and hear, but relate and communicate to and with one another not as "us" versus "them," but as "we," for we all benefit from learning, worshiping, praying, serving, and being in fellowship with one another.[5]

In some arenas of church life this push toward inclusion is occurring. For example, inside academia there are schools that allow people to focus on disability studies, with a push by some to make disability studies part of a seminary curricula under the category of "practical theology." More seminaries are training more people with disabilities to be Ministers of the Word and Sacrament, priests, and other religious leaders, depending upon the denomination and their respective ordination practices.

Yet what is being proposed in this book is the full inclusion of *all* people in the body of Christ, where *all* people are given an opportunity to add their voice, their song, their words, their gestures, their hands, their feet, their presence, and their spirit alongside one another *in* Christ. The challenge is that it will mean new ways of understanding and practicing worship as those who are less articulate or have a harder time focusing for long periods of time will shape our worship of God as we shape each others' habits and practices. Education as teaching people to be disciples will shift significantly as we learn gestures of charity and service to one another in and outside a church. Music and prayers may change as people with disabilities lead and participate in newly constructed choirs that use something as simple as Orff-Kodaly rosewood xylophone bars along with voices and hand bells. Youth group compositions will change significantly, as will preschool and parents' morning out programs as people with developmental disabilities bring their children to church-wide gatherings.

A term that will be further explored and explained in this book is "co-creation," which is a significant part of inclusion. To be included is more than merely being in an office, a classroom, a sanctuary, or fellowship hall. To be included is more than a statistic or quota fulfillment. To be included is more than simply being able to do what the people who are able-bodied decide is acceptable, right, and good in a congregation. To be included means to be considered equals with each other in a parish, to be treated with dignity and respect, just like all the other members of a congregation, just as God perceives us as well. To be included is to be co-creators and collaborators, and to have co-creating opportunities in worship, prayer, education, fellowship, and service with one another.

Consider this book a proclamation and iteration that the body of Christ is an inclusive body.

Beyond Accessibility: The Book's Structure

This book is divided into two parts. Part one focuses on the biblical and theological basis or groundwork for making the argument for inclusivity in the body of Christ. After all, what is unique about this body of believers is that it is the body of none other than the crucified and risen Christ, as the Apostle Paul, and later Karl Barth reminds us. This identification is important for this book for no one is an isolated individual, an "I," in the body of Christ. Instead, we are members connected with one another, mysteriously and wonderfully woven together and in relationship with one another because such is the nature of God in Christ. The Spirit in each of us reminds us that we are known and loved best by Christ, the head of the body, who is known only through the fellowship that we have with one another. The emphasis is always on the "we-ness" or "us-ness" in the body of Christ, for we are all dependent upon the love and grace of Jesus, regardless of whether the world labels us "disabled" or "able-bodied."

Part two is the manual, the "how-to" part of the book, focusing on the moves or phases that may be taken by congregations in becoming or moving toward full inclusion. For example, as has been suggested above, there are opportunities in the life of many churches for educating people with disabilities with specialized Sunday school curricula, along with special times of worship for people with intellectual and developmental disabilities. This is the first step, the essential move forward. In baseball language this is the "first base," of welcoming people with disabilities into the life of a church. Making it possible for people with disabilities to simply have physical and programmatic access into a building or activity is an important act of hospitality.

The problem for the Church is—to continue the baseball analogy— that the church believes it has hit a home run when it has simply gotten to first base. While many churches built in the 1950s, 1960s and 1970s installed elevators and hearing devices (hard black plastic headsets in the front pew in the United Methodist Church I grew up in during the 1960s), more modern "mega-churches" along with newer mainline churches, are designing structures that are mindful of people with disabilities, or at least physical disabilities, along with sensory disabilities. Churches with large screens in the sanctuary provide a way for people who are incapable of holding a hymnal or Bible an opportunity to participate, while others provide a signing interpreter during worship for those who use sign language.

Yet the real challenge is not necessarily providing for people with disabilities the opportunity to worship, be educated, pray, serve, and be in fellowship with one another. The real challenge is leadership and full, open, and voluntary participation with one another in all areas of the church's life, in which people with disabilities are no longer waiting to be asked to be part of the body, but are initiating and taking leadership roles by fully participating in the planning of a Vacation Bible School or by enrolling people to bring food for a church potluck via voice activated email systems. Thus the second section will focus on possible movements toward full inclusion of *all*.

Beyond Accessibility: A Different Kind of Book

Beyond Accessibility is unique in several respects. First, I am writing from the vantage point of being an interim senior pastor in a Presbyterian Church in North Carolina. While I wrote my first book *God Plays Piano Too* from the vantage point of the Director of Religious Life at an institution for children with disabilities, and *Unexpected Guests at God's Banquet* and *Dancing with Disabilities* from my academic offices at Duke University, I admit that writing this book in the context of a living, breathing, changing congregation makes a difference in how I come to this latest project. The writing of this book will be largely personal memoir and sermonic—such is my style of writing, especially as a pastor. The chapters will tend to be more "to the point" and devoid of lots of foot- and end-notes because I have little time to write longer and denser academic essays these days amid writing sermons, newsletters, blogging, pastoral work, and administering a church staff, while also tending to the needs of a family and, as my second job, leading pilgrimages around the world.

As the interim senior pastor of the church that Rich is a member of, I am aware that Rich's church has done all the right and politically correct innovations in terms of making it possible for Rich—or anyone with a physical disability—to physically enter into the Church building from more than one place. There is the sloping entrance into the Fellowship Hall, though the door to the Hall needs the mechanism that causes the door to open automatically by the flip of a switch. Then there is an elevator right off of the sanctuary, with an outside entrance that opens up into the small narthex. There is also one bathroom in the building, directly under the sanctuary, that is "handicap" accessible to which a person can get access by simply going down the elevator.

Also, once in the sanctuary, rather than cutting out the pews in a haphazard pattern, enabling a person with a disability and in a wheelchair or using a walker to sit wherever she or he might want, there are two pews on the front row that are designated for people in wheelchairs. Of course, the joke is this: when was the last time Presbyterians were ever eager to sit in the front row of the sanctuary?

The reality is that this congregation is more progressive than many in making their church physically accessible for people with disabilities. However, the other part of "reality" is that there is so much more that needs to be done: from projectors for showing the words to hymns for those with visual limitations during worship; gluten-free bread for Holy Communion; Braille and Spanish signage in the halls; large print bulletins; accessibility to a signing interpreter for those with hearing impairments; to providing opportunities for people with intellectual disabilities to participate in worship. We need to continue searching for ways that people whom the world calls "disabled" may more openly participate in the life of the body of Christ.

In other words, churches have become more physically accessible to people with disabilities. There are more portals or points of entry—to use a computer term—that people with disabilities may use in order to enter physically into the life of a church. But I am struggling with figuring how the church may be more inclusive of people like Rich.

Second: I am writing this book with the eyes of an outsider to the church myself. As an out-gay man, as well as being an ordained clergyperson in the Presbyterian Church (USA), I come to this book as an outsider, one who has also been marginalized and made to feel like a second class citizen because of simply being who I am. In reading, talking, and sharing stories with people with disabilities over many decades, I know that it is this sense of being a second-class citizen that causes such intellectual headaches, emotional hurt, and spiritual heartache. While the arguments may be different at times—some would argue that being disabled at least has more possibilities of biblical justifications for full inclusion than being gay in this day and age—nonetheless many of our friends have asked for a "miracle healing" that we may be "whole" one day . . . whatever "whole" looks, feels, and sounds like.

Third: this book will hopefully push us all toward figuring out how we are to live with one another in the body of Christ in a post-disabled ministry context. In other words, I am proposing a day and age when there will no longer need to be "Disability Ministry Sundays," with special music and liturgies in worship, or the need to highlight that people with disabilities are still not a part of church leadership, let alone membership. I am predisposed to understanding inclusion as enclosure, in which the image before me is the Spirit bringing us all together into the same room—perhaps a sanctuary—and then locking the doors behind us and saying, "O.K. live with each other with what you have and who you are." We, created in God's image, are all on the same ship of faith, learning what it is to be a disciple with one another as Christ instructed. The Church is not another episode of a reality television show, in which each week the majority throws out a member of the body. Rather, we are drawn more tightly together in the body of Christ, just as we are, because of who and whose we are.

To this end, people with disabilities and people who are able-bodied will need to accommodate and change as we shape, challenge, nurture, question, confront, comfort, and love one another, just as Christ's Spirit would want us to live as members of this amazing body.

A Show of Hands

After worship each Sunday in Henderson, North Carolina, I would go out to a local restaurant with a group of women and men from my church. Going to the restaurant has replaced going home to cook for many of us in the church. In our discussions about this book, we had a wonderful discussion about who is able and disabled in the body of Christ by a showing of hands. One member of our group held up her hand that is missing a tip of the finger that was cut off earlier in life. Another member held up her arthritic hand that she is not able to place flat upon a tabletop anymore, with the prospect that in the future her hand will only become more constricted. There were hands with liver spots, short nails, long nails, rings on fingers, and no rings. What I learned from this show of hands is the uniqueness of each of our lives, whether we had full usage of our hands or not. Nevertheless, we were all members of the body of Christ, each of us with our different hands, making the body more unique and special than anyone ever thought.

Notes

1. Multiple Sclerosis is a disease of the central nervous system, which is the white matter of the brain and the spinal cord that affects any or all of the various systems and subsystems of the nervous system. Writer Nancy Mairs, who lives with MS, further describes it as affecting "everything from whether your eyes can steadily follow a moving finger to whether your toes curl under when a sharp object scrapes along the sole of your foot." However, this does not mean that the cortex is affected, leaving many people with MS physically incapacitated, but able to think clearly. See Nancy Mairs, *Waist High in the World* (Boston: Beacon Press, 1996), 27.

2. I put quotation marks around the word "community of people with disabilities" because I think there is about as much a sense of "community" as there are among people who are lesbian, gay, bisexual, transgender, or questioning. In other words, such communities are more diverse and heterogeneous than homogeneous. But by being labeled or categorized as living with a "disability" or being "gay," one is suddenly lumped together with a group of other people, along with all the stereotypes and one-dimensional caricatures that are applied to them.

3. A word about language: being "disabled" is but the latest rhetorical shift taken in the "name game" of people with disabilities. It is highly important to use "people first" language, because, first, it emphasizes the "person" who is not only disabled, but is also a mom, a dad, a son, a daughter, an artist, writer, or

theologian. Secondly, the term "handicap" is a throwback to a time and place in which the "handicapped" assumed the begging gesture of putting one's cap in the hand and asking for alms for the victim. To this day, even in disability studies, there are people who will not use "person first" language. Third: to complicate things even more, "disability" fails to capture the nuances of a person's limitations. For example, a person with Down syndrome may be very "able-bodied," because his or her body works and is able to move with no problems. Thus, is the person living with Down syndrome disabled? Or do they have an intellectual or developmental limitation? Furthermore, people who cannot hear may understand themselves not to be "disabled" per se, but are part of a group called "deaf culture" in which those who associate with deaf culture do not understand themselves as "disabled." For this book, I will use the language of "person" or "people with disabilities," and "people who are non-disabled" or "persons who are able-bodied."

4. Again, there is no homogeneous group known as the "disability community" in which there is a common understanding and ground of being. It is a diverse and eclectic group, and I use this term "community" loosely.

5. This is explored further in the Presbyterian Church (USA) Advisory Committee on Social Witness Policy paper, "Living Into the Body of Christ: Toward Full Inclusion of People with Disabilities," approved in 2006, of which I was the main author.

CHAPTER TWO

The Church:
The Body of Christ

There is one body and one Spirit, just as you were called to the one hope of your calling. —EPH. 4:4.

For just as the body is one and has many members, and all the members of the body, though many, are one body, so it is with Christ. —1 COR. 12:12.

You are the body of Christ —1 COR. 12:27.

My Uncle Willie and the Segregation of People with Disabilities

In my decades of work with people with disabilities in various faith communities, I am often asked why I am invested in the cause. Here is one of the reasons: because a member of my extended family would have been considered mentally retarded, developmentally delayed, or intellectually challenged.

Uncle Willie was my grandmother's brother. He was slightly slower in processing social nonverbal cues and speech, and seemed to live a simple life with my grandparents who cared for him all the adult years of his life. With fondness, I remember my parents and grandparents engaged in conversation, too busy for us some times, and Uncle Willie taking us on a walk to get some ice cream or candy at a convenience store a block away from our house. There was no doubt that Uncle Willie was loved by all the family members, who cared for and met his needs until the day he died. For Uncle Willie, the community or circle of care was his family. While my Uncle Willie did not live in the day of sheltered workshops per se, or live independently in his own or a shared apartment (though I think he could have), he was always part of a family that loved him unconditionally. I know of other families who, like my own, cared for children, siblings, and more distant relatives who were living with a disability. Along with a network of friends and acquaintances, these families welcomed and cared for *and* were cared for by people with disabilities. As discussed in the introduction to this book, many people with disabilities were either institutionalized or cared for by family members throughout the first half of the twentieth century and before that.

But in a strange way these people with disabilities, who were widely accepted in their family communities, were kept segregated and separated from other venues in the public square, such as employment and education in a public school. Sadly, a third venue where people with disabilities were kept segregated and separated from people who were able-bodied happened to be local faith communities. These included Christian (Protestant, Catholic, and Eastern Orthodox communities), Jewish, Muslim, and other faith communities. In segregating people with disabilities, faith communities were simply following the practices of ordinary life.

Scriptural Resources for Inclusiveness

I began working with people with disabilities when I was sixteen years old. While conducting a project on the historical parts of Portland, Oregon, I met many men and women who were recently discharged from the state institution for people living with a developmental disability or mental illness. Some were burned out Viet Nam war veterans. Many were living in seedy hotel rooms that had seen better days. Today, that part of Portland in which these hotels were located has been gentrified, preserved, and restored, replaced with cute boutiques and fashionable health food stores. The men and women who I first met on the city streets, in run-down hotels, and at missionary storefronts, have moved on to who knows where.

My first job in working with people with disabilities was as a recreation therapist. While still a college student, I worked with young adolescents with developmental disabilities who were living in a retirement-nursing home in Spokane, Washington. Though placement of people with disabilities in a retirement home was perhaps not ideal, the alternative was to place these young women and men in a large, lonely, state institution outside the city limits. Combining elderly people and young people with disabilities into joint projects and outings presented an interesting mix of people. It was clear that they all enjoyed each other's companionship on most days—though there were often complaints from the elderly that the young were moving too fast during trips to the zoo, and vice versa from the young urging those who were older to hurry up to the polar bear exhibit. On weekdays, the young people went to their respective schools, while the elderly stayed at the home. What seemed interesting was, despite all their quirky differences as people and not because of their disabilities per se, they seemed to meld into a kind of serendipitous community.

My work in institutions for people with disabilities began in earnest in my first internship at what was then called the Delaware Hospital for the Mentally Retarded, or HMR for short, as mentioned in the introduction. I was subsequently hired to work as a music therapist at the public school that was on the grounds of the HMR. There was no community per se in this institution. Though there was great camaraderie among the staff, there was no camaraderie among the young people with disabilities, unless there was a birthday party or a celebration of a holiday, when everyone would be brought together.

It was in my work with the young people with disabilities, and the choir I worked with on the grounds of HMR, that I first experienced the awareness of how disconnected the Church—universally and locally—was from the lives of the young people I worked with who were disabled. When I went to pastors, inquiring about the possibilities of bringing the choir to their churches, I was always invited to come to an evening service on Sunday or Wednesday, but never at 11:00 A.M. on Sunday morning. Why? "Because they wouldn't understand what was going on!" said many of the pastors. Some pastors said that the choir members with disabilities weren't welcomed because they might be disruptive at the 11:00 A.M. worship. Instead of attending Sunday services in local churches, the young people thus went to the small chapel on the grounds of HMR on Sunday morning at 11:00 A.M. It was here that I became conscious of the injustice that was taking place, and which I was taking a part in: the exclusion of people with disabilities in this institution from nearby community-based churches. Why? Simply because they were disabled.

I started to discover that this form of segregation was not unusual as I tried to bring the choir to Sunday morning worship services in churches of different denominations around the geographical area, only to discover that there were many more faith communities—Christian, Jewish, and Muslim, to name a few—who were equally "guilty" of excluding people with disabling conditions. It was clear that people with visible disabilities, especially those with certain intellectual and social disabilities, were simply not welcome into these sanctuaries at the beloved 11:00 worship hour. As has been reported elsewhere, especially by African Americans who tried to attend worship in largely white churches, 11:00 A.M. on Sunday morning has become known as the most segregated hour in American society.[1]

The questions that these experiences raised started to come quickly and furiously, and stayed with me throughout my seminary studies, during my work as an assistant Chaplain at Eastern State School and Hospital in Trevose, Pennsylvania, and continuing through three books, numerous essays, sermons, and workshops:

- What was the place and presence of people with disabilities in the context of ancient Jewish community?
- How were people with visible or invisible disabilities treated or viewed by Jesus?
- Were the apostles and the early church welcoming of people with disabilities?

The answers and responses to these questions were, not surprisingly, pointing to the lack of voice or presence of people with disabilities, even though the Scriptures point to a benevolent, if not prophetic, God who sides with and heightens the importance of people with disabilities in the realm, the reign, and the kingdom of God. God in Christ, in the form of the Holy Spirit in our world today, sides with or has a bias and prejudice toward people whom the world calls "disabled." For *all* of human creation, regardless of what a person cannot or can do, is secondary to the primary reason for our being in the first place: God created us to be in relationship with the Holy One and each other.

Proof of this bias is found in the following passages that came to the fore in arguing for the full inclusion of people with disabilities in faith communities, be it Jewish or Christian:

- Isaiah 43: In this prophecy about the restoration and preservation of Israel, God is bringing all nations, gathering all people to give witness to the omnipresence of God. Part of this gathering included people from the north, south, east and west (verses 4–8). But the part that stands out is who else is included in this gathering of God's people:

"Bring forth the people who are blind, yet have eyes, who are deaf, yet have ears! Let all the nations gather together and let the peoples assemble" (Isaiah 43: 8, 9). This passage, and others like it throughout the Old Testament or Hebrew Scriptures, point to the will of God that all people, including those who are disabled in any way, be included in and among the people of Israel.

• Luke 14:15–24: the Parable of the Great Banquet Feast. I wrote another book around this very parable, *Unexpected Guests at God's Banquet*. The main thrust of this "kingdom of God" parable is that people with disabilities have, for a lack of a better phrase, a "front row" seat in the kingdom of God. Add to this stories like the woman with a hemorrhage (Mark 5:25) or the man who is blind (John 9), and we are aware of Jesus' ministry to–and inclusion of–those whom we call today disabled or living with a hidden disease.

Paul's Letters: It is not necessarily what Paul writes, but what he does not write that gives us pause to consider the breadth, depth, and height of those who are considered members of the body of Christ. There is an equaling "out" among the members of the body, in which the world's designation or labeling of Jew or Greek, slave or free, male or female (Gal. 3:28) is no longer important. Nor is there gay or straight, able-bodied or disabled. What is key is that we are all one in Christ Jesus (Gal 3:29); that is, all secondary or humanly constructed labels, designations, and categories vanish because of the incorporation of all Christians into Christ's body through "one Spirit."

In sum, if it is God's desire, God's will, and God's hope that *all* of us are called to be part of the realm of God's love and to be members of the communion of the saints on earth and above–with Jesus teaching us to pray that God's will be done, "on earth as it is in heaven" (Matt. 6:10)–then the challenge before us is twofold: first, how do we imagine this gathering of God's people called "church"? Is it the building we go to, or the people who gather in God's name? Second, if we are currently not living the Gospel vision, the Jesus-life–if we are living with a segregation of people who are able-bodied versus persons with disabilities in the body of Christ–then how do we move toward living in the more inclusive nature of God's love and of God's realm on earth, with the template of the heavenly gathering as our guide?

The remaining part of this chapter examines the nature of the Church as the body of Christ. While there are several other ways, other metaphors and analogies, that we can use to study and understand the

Church—from a flock of sheep (John 10:11–16), to vines and branches (John 15:105)—the one vision that seems a major image in many of Paul's letters, repeated time and again (Romans, 1 Corinthians, Colossians, Ephesians), is the body of Christ. Why? Because, at first glance, we are addressing the issue of those whom society calls dis-abled (meaning literally not able or lacking ability), which includes those who are un-able to move, think, reason, feel, or sense the world as the supposed majority do.[2] Until we get to know one another, we are unaware of the incredible gifts and talents, indeed strengths of character that are often hidden, even to the person living with a disability. We all have physical, bodily, intellectual, relational, and spiritual limitations, where we are not as "able" as others might be. Therefore, we are all dependent upon one another, and especially relying on Jesus, who alone is able to carry us through each day of our lives. So let us consider the Church as the body of Christ, a body with many members, yet one head, Jesus Christ. We Christians believe that the Church began with Jesus Christ himself, who gave us the Church, and showed us the contours, practices, virtues, and subsequently sacraments of the Church as he preached and lived the Good News. In light of his sacrificial death, resurrection, and presence among us today, we are inheritors of the grace of God through faith. Christ now lives in us, and we live in Christ. This gift makes it possible for us to be part of the body of Christ, or in another image, makes us members of the household of God whose foundation includes the gathering of apostles and prophets, "with Christ Jesus himself as the cornerstone. In him the whole structure is joined together and grows into a holy temple in the Lord, in whom you also are built together spiritually into a dwelling place for God" (Eph. 2:20–22).

This body of Christ is not like any other human body, as theologian Karl Barth reminds us. This is none other than Jesus Christ's body, the risen Son of God, the new Adam, in and with whom we encounter God through fellowship and community with other Christians. Barth understood that Christ's body is not a human body but is a kind of reflective realism; that is, the Church as Christ's body *reflects* attributes of the human body without being identical to Christ's body.[3] Ronald Rohlheiser reminds us that Paul never tells us that the body of believers replaces Christ's, nor that it represents Christ's body, nor even that it is Christ's mystical body. God is still here, just as real and physical as God was in Jesus Christ. If it is true that we are members of Christ's body, then God's presence in the world today depends very much on us.[4]

Gerhard Lohfink reminds us that when the Apostle designates us, the Church, as the body of Christ, there is an educational agenda in Paul's writing: he wants us to be and learn to become the body of Christ. Saying that we are the "body of Christ" does not mean that we are equal to the living Word, his life, his purity, and his total surrender. Rather, we, who are members of the body, are challenged to constantly consider and reconsider what it means to live with one another, understanding our place before the omniscient God of creation, *and* the members of the living, breathing, moving, transforming presence of Christ in the Church.[5]

Characteristics of the Body of Christ

More specific characteristics of the body of Christ speak directly to the place and presence of people with disabilities:

The Microcosm Reflects the Macrocosm

The local church or parish that we attend and in which we participate— whether it be a baptism, marriage or civil union, or gathering together for worship, fellowship, service, and education—reflects and is part of the divine mystery of the body of Christ. While there are times that our local congregation may feel and look more like the menagerie of characters from Maurice Sendak's *Where the Wild Things Are*, by grace, with the water of baptism as a sign and seal of all that God has done, is doing, and will do, we are part of the ever expanding, always divine yet incredibly human, body of Christ.[6]

Paul's description of the church as the body of Christ, using the image of "body," was nothing new in his day and age. Biblical scholars Dale Martin and Peter Brown write extensively on the many ways that the word "body" was used in those days to talk about a greater political group of people, a "body" of people. Athens and Rome were and had such a "body politic." Dale Martin writes that the body, according to ancient Jewish and Greek sources, was a microcosmic reflection of the macrocosm which it was part of and surrounded by, namely the universe, with cosmic dust and all.

Likewise, the body of Christ, located in and on a local congregation or parish, is both a reflection of and made of the very same "matter" or breathes the same Spirit as the other parts of the greater, universal, and yet mysterious body of Christ. Indeed, the early Greeks assumed that human bodies themselves were made of the same "stuff" or matter as the world around them, such as air, earth, water, and fire. Thus the body of Christ on a congregational level is a microcosmic synthesis of the larger macrocosmic body of Christ, in which we are made of the same "stuff" as Christ himself.[7] In other words, in true Trinitarian fashion, the Holy Spirit is also God's Spirit, and Christ's Spirit is also in us, and we in God (John 14).

Macrocosmic talk can be overwhelming to our senses. In order to wrap our small minds around the reality that we are called by God to live, it is helpful and it makes more sense to talk about the body of Christ's members on the level of congregations and parishes, namely what we engage in weekly if not daily. We are going to find those who are literally and figuratively the "eyes," the "toes" or the "ears" in the body of Christ (whether one is considered disabled or non-disabled), not in some other cosmos, but on the level of congregational life, in persons seated next to us or behind us. After all, where else do we learn the art and practice of serving one another—teaching, preaching, and caring for each other—but in the one-to-one, ongoing, good-days-and-bad-days relationships we have with one another in our daily lives in our local faith communities?

The Head of the Body Is Christ

There is an order in this body of Christ, even in the churches of the Reformed traditions and their democratic ways of living and making decisions. While the body members may have a kind of equality with one another, there is also a hierarchy in which the physical body, like the spiritual body, takes its cues from the head of the body as the primary seat of knowledge. Plato believed that the human head is spherical because that is the shape of divinities, and that the head, being the most divine part of the body, ruled the rest. In fact, the ancient world considered the body to be a mere vehicle for the head, designed to carry it and keep it from rolling around on the ground.

Paul writes about the head of the body being Christ, in which the rest of the body takes its cues. In Ephesians we read: "we must grow up in every way into him who is the head, into Christ, from whom the whole body, joined and knit together by every ligament with which it is equipped, as each part is working properly, promotes the body's growth in building itself up in love" (Eph. 4: 15, 16).

The only way we can discern the thoughts and cues of the mind of Christ is by our discussions, relationships, and meetings with each other, whether in worship or in the side aisle of a grocery store. Some may do it with sign language, others by reading lips, still others by playing a game of baseball with a ball that makes noise so that a person who is blind can play. It is in the games of life, in the worship of community, in fellowship, in prayer together, in discussions on critical issues, and in silence, that we discern the will, the mind, of Christ.

The Porous, Permeable Nature of the Body of Christ

In order for the Holy Spirit to move within the body of Christ and among its members, there needs to be a certain permeable or porous boundary between the Spirit and us, the body.

In the ancient world, there is the idea of balance and harmony, in which there are permeable boundaries in all bodies, physical and social alike. Because our physical and social bodies are a part of the universe we live in, we are constantly influenced by the elements in it. Physically, it is through the pores of the skin that our bodies breathe by absorbing and expelling, taking in and sweating out, sustaining our internal organs in an important balance or equilibrium. The pores help serve as a part of the human thermometer system, in which, when we are overheated, we sweat, and which, when we are cold, our pores tighten. There is no firm boundary between us and nature: our skin's pores help keep the body healthy.

Likewise, the body of Christ and its members are porous. In order for the Spirit of God to move freely within this social body, the Spirit needs entry into our lives. Indeed, in order that we may share the same breath of God, and grow in the gifts, talents, and services bestowed upon the body, the body of Christ must be porous: "To one is given through the Spirit the utterance of wisdom, and to another the utterance of knowledge, according to the same Spirit" (1 Cor. 12:8). This happens through the Spirit's movement in the daily life of the members of the body of Christ, both people who are able-bodied and people who are disabled together.

The Holy Spirit

What seeps into and through the very flesh of our being, and the porous-like nature of the body of Christ, is the Spirit. Again, coming from the world of the ancient Greeks, *pneuma* or Spirit was the "stuff" of life itself, making it possible for the human body to move and have sensation. The very air we breathe in and out is filled with the "stuff" of life, which includes the Spirit.

Likewise, for the Church it is the Holy Spirit who makes it possible for us not only to live as Christ's body, but also to move and proclaim with lips, hands, feet, arms, head, and torso that: "Jesus is Lord only by the Holy Spirit" (1 Cor. 12:3).

The Spirit is important in our discussion about the place and presence of people with disabilities in the body of Christ. Paul Wilkes writes that in the act of discerning our place, role, and function in the body of Christ, discerning the Holy Spirit is not only an act of cognition, but is "available to those who are able to open their hearts to God. Our minds can sort out the details later, but without this opening, the power of the Holy Spirit. . . cannot enter our lives." Then quoting Pierre de Caussade, Wilkes writes: "God's plans, disguised as they are, reveal themselves to us through intuition rather than through our reason."[8]

What is crucial in our reading from 1 Corinthians about the Spirit, and the centrality of Spirit in the body of Christ, is that Paul writes that the Spirit, which is God, decides what gift, talent, and service we bring to the body of Christ. And in Scriptures, the Spirit is not aware of the same labels and categories—particularly able-bodied or disabled—as is the modern Church. In other words, the Spirit decides what gifts, talents, and services we bring to the membership of the body of Christ that is located in our congregation or parish.

Many Members

In the world of the "Me-Generation," that selfishly follows its own "bliss" and praises individual choice and freedom, there has been a strident tone in people choosing to do whatever pleases them, and the rest of us, well, "who cares?"

The "Me-Generation" (which has also been called the Y-Generation or iPod-Generation) is in direct contrast to the plurality and diversity of the one, united body of Christ. In Paul's general description of the body of Christ there are many parts or members that make up the body, "yet not all the members have the same function, so we, who are many are one body in Christ, and individually we are members one of another" (Rom. 12: 4, 5).

Consider Paul's first letter to the church in Corinth, in which he writes "Now *you* are the body of Christ and individually members of it" (12:27). I've italicized the *"you"* in this passage for a reason: I've learned in the South what the ancient Greeks meant in sometimes using "you" singular, and "you" plural. In this case, Paul was writing and using the "you" plural here as in "y'all." In other words, "Y'all are the body of Christ." Each person in a congregation or parish is a member of this collection of all kinds and sorts of people: short, tall, thin, stout, healthy, slightly under the weather, rich, poor, gay, lesbian, straight, young, old, teenager. . . everyone.

Again: the beauty of this plurality is that we know God personally and only through relationships, through fellowship with one another. One friend, when visiting Catholic churches in which he was not a member, would sit next to a perfect stranger because he knew that as long as he remained sitting by himself he would not come to know God in that context. It is in shaking hands, embracing one another, flashing the "Peace" sign during the passing of the peace, singing with each other (whether on or off-key), playing a musical instrument in worship, joining in coffee or punch after or before worship in a fellowship hall, greeting one another when entering and leaving a body of people who are praying or in worship, that we know God, and we are known by God. That is why we are created to be social, relational beings; we only come to know who and whose we are in the context of others around us, be it in the context of living in a family or in a faith community. The writer Richard Rohr states it perfectly: "Would we be so arrogant to say that all the preceding centuries of Christians and Jews have not also known, listened to and followed the Lord?"[9] Rohr continues: ". . . we stand on the shoulders of all the wise persons and saints of the past. Some historical accidents have been facilely passed on as universal tradition, yet are not the consistent coherent pattern. So we need the body (of Christ) to keep us beyond cultural arrogance and tied to *all* the ancestors. We can't each start from zero."[10]

Not only are there many members upon whose shoulders we rest upon, there are also those who do the work of the Gospel among us, this very day. Richard Rodriguez writes that we are part of a new community "who share with each other daily the experience of standing alone with God."[11] In the body of Christ we are constantly looking out for the needs of other people first rather than necessarily thinking of ourselves and our own self-centered needs This may mean that we are members one of another in the body, not writing our own story, but writing our story with others who are with us now and who will follow us.

A Healthy Dependency

Richard Rodriguez posed the following descriptive difference between Protestants and Catholics: Protestants are a confederation or a loose gathering of individual "I's," who stand around together as a church, bumping into each other only if they have to, whereas Catholicism is the singular collection of the "I." In Protestantism, the "I's" exist with one another, tolerating certain differences and eccentricities, but don't want to get into each other's family business too much, while the Catholics cannot help but be involved in everyone's business.

In the body of Christ, we are continually learning and re-learning the lesson of the "we-ness" of the corporate nature of our shared existence. Living corporately is a daunting daily challenge because in the world around us, there is the tendency for the larger society to lift up and glorify the individual "I." But in doing so, we may find ourselves easily forgetting the "we" who brought up each and every one of us, for the good and for the bad.

Here's an example of the power and the importance of the "we" versus the "I" in the church. A friend muttered several years ago when passed over for the glorious MacArthur "Genius" grant, that the award perpetuates the fallacy that it is given to an individual when in truth it took an entire network of friends, family members, and people in the past to made it possible for the singular individual to be here today, exercising his or her gifts. No one is truly sui generis, or in other words a genius by him- or herself. After all, there are those who taught the now dubbed "genius"—whether it be how to think, feel, write, sing, dance, do mathematical equations, draw, paint, and scramble an egg—who are not being figured in the prize. As the African proverb states truthfully, "it takes a village." In other words, no one is a genius by him- or herself.

It has been my experience that people with a disabling condition have often helped a "gathering of individual I's" become a "we." There will be more about this later in the book, but suffice it to say that one of the reasons faith communities need the presence of people whom the world calls "disabled" is because they enable or facilitate the group in becoming a community. By their mere presence, they represent the immediacy of mortality. Let me explain: I hear often a person who views him- or herself as non-disabled say that, by simply being in the presence of someone who is disabled, they begin to struggle with a sense of their own disability or impending loss of abilities. That sudden awareness creates a bond between a person who is non-disabled with a person who is disabled. The "I" of the disabled person and the "I" of the able-bodied person are no longer separate individuals; they are a "we" who share the same mortality and eventual loss of abilities.[12]

We also share a dependency not only upon one another but also upon God in Christ. Perhaps this is the true equalizer: everyone—whether a person is able-bodied or disabled—is dis-abled, literally not able-to do or be something or be someone, and is totally dependent upon the gift of grace through faith. Likewise, everyone is dependent upon the living examples of Jesus' ministry in order to figure out how we are to live together in the body; everyone is dependent upon the stories of the Old and New Testament to know where we've been as a people, where we are, and where we are headed. And everyone is dependent upon gifts of hospitality, of welcome, of acceptance just as we are, with full inclusion in the body of believers. All human creatures are dependent creatures, from our birth to our death, and beyond.

But there is another, deeper, level by which we are dependent upon each other within the body of Christ.[13] In working among, being in worship with, playing around, and going to the hospital with people with disabilities, I've slowly learned that, at times, while I may not be physically able to be at certain places or do certain parts within a family or congregation, others are able to be present and do what I cannot do. And do so in my name, which is almost as good as my doing it myself. Others represent me and others who cannot be present for whatever the reason may be. For example, a United Methodist pastor, the late Rev. Susan Allred, liked to tell her congregation that when she would visit the hospital, she would often tell the person she was visiting, "I'm here representing Parker, Adrianne, John, Mary, Theodore, and Barbara, who were not able to be here today, but they are part of the fellowship of Christ's disciples that you are part of, and they wanted to be remembered to you." Yet at other moments, when a friend is in deep depression and not able to believe necessarily in a loving God amid the *Sturm and Drang* of life, I can be directly present in that period of darkness in my friend's life, holding the other person in my arms, carefully tending to one's needs and wants, bringing him or her what is needed, and guarding him or her from all hurt and harm to the best of my abilities.

Vulnerability leads to an intimate sense of the community of Christ as we all confess or concede that none of us as individuals are either Superman or Wonder Woman and that we are unable to be in all places, and to be all things to all people. But we can do amazing things when we are part of community, who do these things in Christ's name. For example, I used to teach a class about the virtue of dependency by standing at one end of the room, and pointing to a cup of water at the opposite end. I told the class I could touch the cup without moving from my spot, but only with their help. We would then all join hands, and the person nearest the cup would touch it. Thus, beginning with my touch, and through the hands of my brothers and sisters, I touched the cup in this link of hands and arms joined together. I stopped touching the cup when hands and arms were let go.

So it is with a person with a disability. While some people may not be able to do certain functions or play a certain role within the body of Christ, in the name of the person with a disability—as well as a person who is not-disabled—we can share in the effort to be present, in that person's name, to play that role or function in a body of believers. After all, no person is an island unto him- or herself, especially in the body of Christ.

Male and Female, God Created Them (Gen. 1:27)

This is a point that will be repeated often in this book: the secondary, humanly created, invented, and maintained labels, categories, and classifications that we use everyday to pigeon-hole, stereotype, and shun people are not primary in the purview of the Creator.

The evidence for this claim is in both 1 Cor. 12:13: "For in the one Spirit we were all baptized into one body—Jews or Greeks, slave or free—and we were all made to drink of one Spirit," and in Gal. 3:28: "There is no longer Jew or Greek, there is no longer slave or free, there is no longer male and female; for all of you are one in Christ."

While the categories of slave and free, Jew and Greek, were pertinent to crises in the days of Paul's writing, and highly important to the communities that Paul was writing to, for the purposes of this book it is important to understand that in the body of Christ there is no longer disabled or able-bodied, young or old, rich or poor, gay or straight, African American, Asian American, or Hispanic- American.

The Last Shall Be the First

The last characteristic of the body of Christ will be covered in the next chapter, namely that the gifts, talents, and services that are necessary for the body of Christ to operate, to exist, and to function, are liberally given out by the Spirit to people within the body, *regardless* of the way that we, who are able-bodied or disabled, may designate these gifts, talents, and services. As has been said often in many biblical study classes, it is obvious, once you search through Scripture, that God chooses the least likely people to be at the right place, at the right time, among the right people, to push forward with the next chapter and verse of God's ongoing story. God chose Noah, a person with a drinking problem, to build an ark to save a world of living things; God chose Jacob, who wounded emotionally his brother Esau and who later himself walked with a physical disability, to become father of great sons; God chose Moses, who had a speech disorder, to lead the people of Israel to their promised land; God chose Ruth, who was not an Israelite, to continue the lineage that would make possible Jesus.

Notes

1. Granted, some churches now meet at 10:00 A.M., but it is noteworthy that many children are also not allowed in certain parts of worship in that hour and are thus segregated from worship with adults, as are many people who are lesbian, gay, bisexual or transgender, who do not feel that they are welcome to come to worship at that hour in most churches.

2. Understand that the world's largest minority group is the heterogeneous group known as "people with disabilities." It is an identity that intersects among all other cultural groupings based on gender, sexual orientation, class, age, race, ethnicity, religion, nationality, and any other humanly created categories or cultural groupings. No one group is immune from a disabling condition.

As I've also noted in my previous books, all disabilities are, in and of themselves, to be understood as a "context dependent" term. In other words, a context (group of people) decide what is or isn't a disability. For example, in American modern society, wearing glasses, contacts, or having eye surgery like laser surgery is not considered by many to be a disability but a fashion statement or accessory. Or in deaf culture, using sign language is not seen as a result of a disability, because being deaf is not a disability in deaf culture. Indeed, the definition or normative description of what is "normal" or "ordinary" keeps shifting according to cultural contexts, and is more fluid that many would consider possible. However what is "normative" is decided upon, it also defines what it is to *not* be normal or disabled.

Another example: watching a group of women or men play rugby in wheelchairs. The only ones who seem abnormal or disabled, and thus not able to play well in a wheelchair, are the people who are called able-bodied and who are standing upright.

3. Brett Webb-Mitchell, *Christly Gestures* (Grand Rapids: Erdmann's, 2003), Part I. I keep returning to the importance of living in the reality that the Church is *the* body of Christ, and I am part of this mystical yet real presence.

4. Ronald Rohlheiser, *Holy Longing* (New York: Doubleday, 2000), 79–80.

5. Gerhard Lohfink, *Does God Need the Church?* (Collegeville: Michal Glazier Press, 1999), 207.

I once had a "Curriculum and Pedagogy of the Church" class session led by a choreographer who directed the class members, "Present your body, mind, and spirit to the living Christ, seated upon this throne," saying this as he threw a chair down in the middle of the circle of students. The bodies of my bright, eloquent students stuttered as they tried to dance and present their lives, with no words, unto God in Christ. We were all quite dis-abled, not as able to dance as we are to argue and talk with and to God.

6. Rev. Jill Edens of United Church of Chapel Hill, North Carolina used this in a sermon on October 11, 2009, and I can't deny it.

7. Peter Brown, *The Body and Society* (New York: Columbia University Press, 1988), 306; Dale Martin, *The Corinthian Body* (Durham: Unprinted manuscript).

8. Paul Wilkes, *Beyond These Walls* (New York: Image, 2000) 118.

9. Richard Rohr, *Radical Grace* (Cincinnati: St. Andrews Press, 1995), 318.

10. Ibid, 318.

11. Richard Rodriguez, *Hunger of Memory* (New York: Bantam, 1983), 110.

12. In this discussion of how people with disabilities may create an ad-hoc sense of community a group of people around an incident around someone's disabling condition, this elicits what are called "do-gooders" who simply cannot seem to help themselves but step in and try to help a person with a disability, whether a person with a disability has said "Yes, you may," or "No, I think I have it under control." Being who we are naturally with one another—whether we are living with a disability or are not—is easier said than done as we slowly put down the masks and costumes of our arbitrary and human-contrived cultural milieu.

13. The word "depend" could also be defined as "to rely upon." While there are times that we find ourselves part of a co-dependent relationship with others in our family, our friendships, acquaintances, and within a congregation or parish—with all its psychological messiness—we do depend upon one another in order to simply live.

CHAPTER THREE

Gifts, Talents, and Services

There are varieties of gifts, but the same Spirit;
varieties of service, but the same Lord;
varieties of activities, but the same God
who activates all of them in everyone. —1 COR. 12:4–6

Each person has a gift to use for the
good and growth of all. —JEAN VANIER[1]

Creator God and Creative Creatures[2]

We are all endowed with the ability to be creative, imaginative, resourceful, and spirited in our zeal to make, form, fashion, and shape the world in which we live.

I begin with this truth, based upon the larger truth that we are all created in the image of God (Gen. 1:27), regardless if one lives with a disability or is non-disabled. As numerous biblical scholars of the Old Testament or Hebrew Scriptures like to remind us, being created in the image of God means that we are created to be in relationship and to be imaginative, albeit with limitations, such as not eating from the tree of knowledge (Gen. 2:17).

The audacious claim in the Old Testament that we are created in the image of God resonates with the focus on the body of Christ that occurs in the New Testament. Up till now in looking at Paul's letters, especially those addressed to the church in Rome, we focused on the truth that we are individually members, one of another, in the body of Christ, and that we are part of a larger gathering of people (Rom. 12:27).

In this chapter, we focus on the corollary proposition that, being created in the image of God, we are also created to be imaginative, creative, talented, remarkable, formidable, and bright people, who share our gifts, talents, and services to the greater, common good of the body of Christ. With the establishment of the "primary relationship" between God and the members of the body of Christ—in which, as creatures of the Creator, there is neither male nor female, Jew nor Greek, slave nor master, able-bodied nor disabled—we are—*all of us*—equally endowed with gifts, talents, and services regardless of the labels or categories that modern society wraps around us. In this chapter, the focus is on the gifts, talents, and services of all people in the body of Christ, *regardless* of what the society around us tells us what we can or cannot do. As Paul wrote: "We have gifts that differ according to the grace given to us" (Rom. 12:6). Below are some examples of gifts that, by God's grace, some people whom the world call "disabled" have to share for the building up and the betterment of the body of Christ

Un-Pretentious Artists among Us

One of the gifts I have received and used throughout my work with people with disabilities, especially people with developmental or intellectual disabilities, is the gift of art, music, and dance. For example, in Morganton, North Carolina, there is a group of men and women, artisans all, who also work together on their art projects at a place called Signature/Studio XI. I enjoy walking into this creative space, with a gallery in the front part of the store, and a workshop area in the back.

Throughout the years I have come to know these talented men and women, who happen to live with a disability. While many of them lived in the nearby institution for a good portion of their lives, many of them have since moved to independent apartments or loosely run group homes, where the people who live in the homes have much leeway. Some of the artists I know have work that has been displayed not only in and around North Carolina, but also in art museums in New York and other large cities, including cities in Europe, like Geneva, Basel, and Amsterdam. The art work is given a special name by the art community, "Art Brut," or primitive or folk art, because the artists were not trained in a standardized or conventional program of an art school. Instead, they were trained by artists who worked in the institutions, and later in studios, who had an appreciation for the artistic process *and* an understanding of what it means to live with a disability in modern society.

What is wonderful about these artists with disabilities is that they are, like all artists, people who have certain styles of painting and who stick to that style of painting, varying little from the style unless pushed, nudged, cajoled, or persuaded by one of the mentor-artists to try doing something different. There is Brooks, a painter who created the cover of my second book, *Unexpected Guests at God's Banquet*,[3] whose illustration shows people at a wonderful banquet feast. His style resembles Grandma Moses', with human beings in stilted, simple poses, against a vast background.

There is also Harold, an artist whom I have followed throughout the years. Harold and Picasso are linked together in style and genre. Harold's cubism and block- like portraits of people, cats, dogs, rocket ships, cars, churches, ministers, parents, and family tableaus, are eerily reminiscent of Picasso. A favorite story narrates Harold thumbing through a book of Picasso's images, pausing, looking up at a friend and asking, "When did I paint these? I don't remember them that well!"
The other artist whose work graces my walls is Ricky Needham. He has moved out of Signature/Studio XI since I first met him a few years ago at an art festival for primitive folk artists at Fearrington Village near Pittsboro, North Carolina. The image I usually hang on my church office walls when I first move in is a profile of Jesus, with long brown hair, manicured beard, and long fingers. Two fingers make the "Peace sign," and Jesus' left eye is watching your every move while a faint smile crosses his lips. This rather hippie-like image of Jesus makes me smile as I imagine Jesus saying something like "Peace, man!" to which the right retort seems to be, "Cool, Dude!"

I remember a songstress who lived with a mental illness and resided close to where the men lived who was also an artist herself who liked to make jewelry in the Studio. I remember other men and women, including staff members, who came and went over the years, some leaving for a new group home or workshop. These individuals always reminded me that they are, first and foremost, artists in their own way, in their own right, and only secondarily that they are people with disabilities. It is hard to call them "disabled" as they are more than able to paint, to sing, to make jewelry, to carve, and to be who God created them to be. They are artists!

Pray Like This . . . With a Twist!

"Pray like this," said Jesus. In the Scriptures, there is an interesting and delightful story of the disciples asking Jesus the simple yet profound request, "Lord, teach us to pray" (Luke 11:1). Jesus taught them the words of what we today call the Lord's Prayer, or what my Catholic friends call the "Our Father."

Throughout the years, I've learned many ways to pray the Lord's Prayer by American Sign Language, in different languages, and with unique practices. For example, the Sisters of St. Benedict's Monastery taught me to pray the Lord's Prayer in a group with the following condition: pray loud enough that you may hear your own voice, but soft enough so that you may hear the two voices on either side of you. Achieving a balance between being loud enough but not too loud softens the voices in prayer and make us all truly listen to the words of the Lord's Prayer.

The other teacher who taught me to pray the Lord's Prayer differently was a young man who lives with cerebral palsy. He is often belted into his wheelchair because of the fear that he will fall because of a seizure. Despite or perhaps because of these limitations, this young man has taught others how to listen deeply to the words of the Lord's Prayer. It has been my experience in many churches—Protestant and Catholic alike—that there is a tendency to utter the words of the Lord's Prayer as fast as possible, with little conscious awareness of what was just prayed. We've repeated the prayer so often that, while God receives the words of our prayers, it is doubtful if we do.

One Sunday morning, we were all caught up in praying the Lord's Prayer quickly, when all of a sudden this young man, with a strong voice, recited the Lord's Prayer with a different cadence. "OUR FATHER, WHICH ART IN HEAVEN, HALL-O-WED BE THY NAME . . ." he prayed loudly . . . and slowly. That's what stopped the rest of the congregation: he prayed it slowly, and with as much articulation as he could muster, given that the muscles of his mouth were not always in synchronicity with his thoughts and feelings.

What happened next was fascinating. After we all stopped, we started to pray the Lord's Prayer differently: we prayed it according to the tempo given to us by this young man. We slowed down the rushed tempo to actually pray each and every word, hearing it as if it were the first time we had ever prayed or heard it. Reciting the prayer that way made all the difference in the world.

And who was our teacher? It was a young man, tied carefully in his wheelchair, who taught us to listen and appreciate every word, as well as the silences between each word prayed. And as we prayed this prayer, we became full of prayer–literally, prayerful–as our lives were transformed into a prayer.

Gifts, Talents, and Services in the Body of Christ

There are countless more stories of people designated "disabled" who are very able and extremely capable of doing amazing things. For example, there is the documentary movie (now available on DVD), *Praying with Lior*. In it, a young man finds that he has a way with praying and prayer unlike others in his community of faith. Even though his father is a rabbi, this does not mean that this ability to pray is genetic. Some people just have the knack, the gift, to pray the right words, at the most propitious moment, lifting a community up when it is grieving over a loss, or a sense of joy.

When living in the l'Arche community in London, England, I was surrounded by women and men who were considered and labeled intellectually challenged, many of whom were also living with disabling conditions like cerebral palsy, mental illness, or the declines associated with old age. Despite these limitations, they were true artisans. There was Brian, a master weaver; and there was the beloved late-Nick, who worked tirelessly in the stone column portion of the workshop. Others in the community simply made a great pot of hot tea at break time, or cleaned up the workshop area without a grumble or groan. Sylvia, Beryl, and Tony were equals in their artistic abilities as well. Their creative, artistic spirit lingers in my very soul as I write this book and look at some of their art in my office, house, and car.

People with disabilities, who have ventured beyond the typical workshop designed for adults with disabilities to embrace the wide swath of what is generically called "the creative arts,"[4] have discovered an untapped wealth of creative, imaginative resources that would have otherwise remained buried without some direct, inspiring intervention. There is no end to moving stories of untapped creative imaginations that are buried deep within a person, especially among those who were thought to have no creativity because they could not talk or communicate easily with others, that come to the surface when a musician, a weaver, a web-designer, a visual artist, a potter, a dancer, or a pantomimist—to name a few talents and gifts of creative expression—bring their art into the world of the one called "disabled." Suddenly, voila, a new talent, a new artist, a new musician, a new art form, is discovered and is born.

As is true in the creative arts, in which artists who express themselves with inventive acts of wonder are audacious souls, the very same kind of creative and courageous people are behind the self-advocacy and self-determination movements in disability-rights communities and gatherings. Without these movements, people with various so-called disabilities would have been shunted to the sidelines of life in the public square or in faith communities. These people now are telling their stories and expressing their ideas in creative, bold, challenging, artistically audacious ways. They are throwing down the gauntlet on what is considered "ordinary" and "status quo." They are not going to live or be in the world as others would expect . . . and want. No longer are people with disabilities asking permission to be present, let alone to express what is on their minds or in their hearts. A new voice is heard: poetry slam performances by people with disabilities raise issues that cause discomfort among people who are able-bodied; sign language is normative and no longer a quaint skill; and wheelchair dancers dance in protest movements.

Again, in the world of "me-ness" where we are given permission to focus solely on ourselves without considering others within a community, it is important to remember that the gifts we have, the talents we employ, and the service we give and receive in a community of faith are not a result of our own doing or creation. It is a result of God's gift of grace. An unbroken thread of grace runs through our art, gift, talent, and service. God has imbued each person with a purpose in life, creating and calling us to be part of Christ's body by being who we were created to be when our names were written in the book of life (also see Ps. 139:13 and God as the Divine knitter, an artistic vision in and of itself). Daily we discover the gifts and services that we all have. And it is among the community of Christians who have known us for a long time—be it in good times or moments of great challenge—that we discover, and often rediscover, what we bring to the body of believers, whether the world labels us "able-bodied" or "disabled."

Remembering the Source

A healthy ego is often necessary for knowing the true source of the gifts we bring with us into the body of Christ. John Howard Yoder reminds us that, when we realize that we depend on God for the gifts and services accorded to us, it is inappropriate to have selfish pride. And pride is always dangerous to the well-being of the life of a community.[5] It is humbling to realize that our gifts and services come entirely through God's grace rather than being based on our own human effort. God delights to see where we go with the grace and inspiration that is sown within the marrow of our bones. *The Rule of St. Benedict* says that it is only in humbling ourselves that we arrive at the "heavenly heights," and that we go down by praising ourselves.[6] In the end, a healthy sense of self, with a dash of humility, is probably best for one and all.

To read or hear that one needs to remember the source of the gift, especially for those just discovering and expressing their abilities, may seem counterproductive. As one person shared with me at a conference, "The last thing we who are disabled want is another crutch or prosthetic device just as we are coming into our own! Your God is a crutch that is not a help, even in my time of need." It seems at times people with disabilities are being told to be humble when humility has been their burden. Yet, remembering the source of our gifts can also be helpful for establishing a healthy sense of self, for God's Spirit is an ever-flowing stream of inspiration, guidance, and self-respect.

What makes achieving this healthy balance of self respect and humility especially challenging for many people with disabilities is that we live in a world where people with disabilities are made to feel and think of themselves as second-class citizens. Many people with disabilities have been kept away from communities of faith, simply because they are disabled, and not because of anything they have done or not done. This is a great injustice, sown and nurtured for generations of people who, most of the time, literally did not know better . . . and in some cases did know better but failed to act. Some times that injustice is outside of the Church, and sometimes it is perpetuated by those within the Church. After years of neglect, if not abuse, from within the body of Christ for and among people with disabilities, there may be the need for a time of truth, reconciliation, and healing.

It might be troubling for some to read the previous paragraph because of the sinful and unjust way some people with disabilities feel and think they have been treated, through no fault of their own. Some times the sense of being treated unjustly simply comes because of the lack of information some people in a congregation have about a person with a disabling condition. This very ability to sense intuitively or know cognitively that there is an injustice, knowing what is right or wrong in a given situation, is something that more and more people with disabilities are speaking out about. Herein lies the problem: On the one hand, many people with disabilities are coming into their own, not with the support of the greater community of faith but by their own sheer will, drive, and desire. So to read or hear that one needs to remember that the source of the gifts one has is not because of one's own abilities or authorship but God's may frustrate a person who is just discovering his or her abilities when the Church was silent and non-supportive in helping one identify one's gifts. On the other hand, simply recognizing the Source can also be helpful, for God's Spirit is an ever-flowing stream of inspiration, a source of guidance when writer's block or artist's block takes hold. As one person shared with me at a conference, "The last thing we who are disabled want is another crutch or prosthetic device just as we are coming into our own! Your God is a crutch that is not a help, even in my time of need." Again, after years of neglect, if not abuse, from within the body of Christ for and among people with disabilities, there may need to be some time for truth, reconciliation, and healing.

Every Member Is Given a Gift

The Holy Spirit has given every member of the body of Christ a gift, or *charisma*, literally meaning grace-given.[7] And every gift is of equal dignity and worth within the body of Christ. The deeper mystery of Christ's body, in which we are baptized by the one Spirit—women and men, poor and rich, disabled and non-disabled, gay and straight, young and old, of all ethnic heritages and nationalities—is that we are all bearers of God-given gifts and services, whatever they may be, for the good of Christ's body (1 Cor. 12).

John Howard Yoder is adamant about this sense of giftedness: the goal of the body of believers in our congregations is to aid others in discovering, naming, owning, and growing into the gift we have been given. We are and are becoming a Church that embraces a Pauline vision of "every-member empowerment," where there would be no one who is not discovering their gift, no one who is not called, no one who is not empowered, and no one who is dominating any other person in the body.[8]

The emphasis on the gifts, talents, and services that we have been given, focusing on the authorship of these attributes within the body of Christ, draws attention to the Giver of the gifts. There is to be a deep acknowledgement of giving praise to the Giver. Yet in doing so, we change our posture as well, from one of living independently to one of healthy dependency as we praise the source of all gifts.[9]

With all this talk of each person discovering one's God-given gift and talent, it is important to stress the need for balance between the individual honing her or his gifts and the common good of the entire community of faith. The Benedictine writer Joan Chittister reminds us that the art of community life is finding the balance of the needs of each person with the needs of a group. By that, she means that there needs to be a balance of the self-giving to the community, but also self-development. After all, the individual person does not exist for a group; rather, a group exists for the good of a person. And it is for the good of the group, like the body of Christ, that we have been given gifts of grace.

In other words, for people with disabilities as well as people who are non-disabled, we need to maintain the balance of both feeding and developing our gifts, perfecting our talents, and being stretched in the art of bearing forth our services unto one another. Yet we do so with our eyes on the larger prize of the good of the community, the body of Christ where we serve God in Christ who lives in the lives of our neighbors, strangers, friends, and family members.

This is easier said or written than done. Such a balancing act is not set once and for all. Balancing the needs of the community and the individual is a challenge for we are more or less spending most of our time out of balance than in synchronicity. It is through conversations, relationships, discussions, silence, presence, hopefulness, ability to appreciate conflict and live through crises, knowing what the balance "is" in our very bones, that we achieve, though only momentarily, this sense of equilibrium. And the act of finding equilibrium begins every morning of every day for the rest of our lives.

Beyond Appearances

As hinted above in this chapter, and to be covered extensively in the next part, *all* people in the body of Christ—regardless of what *we* think or perceive as a person's attributes or possible gifts, talents, or services—are gifted. The Holy Spirit decides with whom the grace-given gift is to be located and in what ways it is to be expressed in the body of Christ. After all, God perceives what we are capable of doing better than we do ourselves.

For example, consider the story of David before he became King of Israel. While Samuel was searching for which son of Jesse would be the next king of Israel, and finding no luck among those that Jesse thought were best fitted for the position, the Lord said to Samuel and Jesse: "Do not look on his appearance or on the height of his stature, because I have rejected him; for the Lord does not see as mortals see; they look on the outward appearance, but the Lord looks on the heart" (1 Sam. 16:7). When all others had been brought before Samuel, Jesse was asked, "Are all your sons here?" and Jesse's retort was, "There remains yet the youngest, but he is keeping the sheep." In other words, Jesse failed to see that his youngest was the one that God had chosen. Jesse failed to see David's heart. And with that, David was brought out of the sheepfold and was anointed by Samuel with the horn of oil, in the presence of his brothers, and the spirit of God came "mightily upon David from that day forward" (1 Sam. 16:13).

God does not look on our outward appearance, our height, our stature, our politics, our gender, our outward abilities, our sexual orientation, our color of skin, our ethnicity, our national heritage, our economic class, our favorite teams (name your sport), or where we live—none of that matters to God. When God wants something done, God chooses, God decides, God directs us, God bestows upon us through faith by grace, what we need to do the work, the action, which God wants done. As reflected in the Pauline letters, God deigns to create us, give us gifts, talents, and services, and then sends each and every one of us into the world to do and be the work of God, and the rest is really history.

Herein lies the trick: to our human eyes, ears, and all other senses, how we judge or assess what a person's gifts, talents, and services are in the greater body of Christ may often times be limited by our own set of experiences. For example, take the list of gifts that differ according to the grace given to us (Romans 12:6–8). When we read that someone is gifted in prophecy, "in proportion to faith," we assume that the person has the ability to write, read, and speak out—just like Amos, Hosea, Jeremiah, Isaiah, Micah, and the rest of the prophets. But is it not possible for someone whom the world might call "disabled" to be prophetic with a paintbrush, clay, or metal, creating a message through artistic mediums that shakes a church, a community, and a world? Is it not possible that a person who is skilled in music but may be blind or visually impaired, or deaf like Beethoven, is able to create music that sets the world afire in telling truth about friendship?

Or what of a teacher of Christian virtues—like self-control or charity—who also happens to be a person who is severely or profoundly disabled? For example, I sent many young seminarians from Duke Divinity School to work at a nearby institution for people with intellectual and other disabilities. Why? Because I wanted to see if the people with intellectual disabilities could teach what I could not teach these young people: the contours of their heart, metaphorically speaking. Here's the situation: Some young seminarians were all "mind," or all about "head knowledge," and did not display any kind of virtue or fruit of the Spirit, like patience, forgiveness, self-control, or charity. After a year's internship at these institutions, many of these very savvy seminarians would come and tell me "thanks," even though they put up the fiercest defense in not wanting to be sent to that institution. Lo and behold, the young seminarians' hearts were changed. I owe many people whom the world calls "disabled" gratitude for their unspeakable gift of teaching others to slow down and consider others in this life.

In terms of givers, in spending time in the local YMCA, I watch as members of a group home, all of whom are living with one kind of disability or another, either check out with their group home assistant or with each other which fitness machine they want to get on before choosing them for themselves. There is a kind of self-giving, of thinking of others, that is not shared with the younger college co-eds who also fill the fitness area of the YMCA. What I witness is a gift of generosity that we can all learn from.

Or another way of stating this is through the body part description found in Paul's first letter to the Corinthians: we are each given a gift, a talent, a service *through* and *by* and *according to* the one Spirit, God, activated by the same Spirit, God, who "allots to each one individually just as the Spirit chooses" (1 Cor. 12: 4–11). Again, each one of us, whether the world calls us able or disabled, is an integral part of the body. Some are given the ability to be an ear to hear the voices of those oppressed, even though they are deaf and use sign language to communicate with the world. Another person is a hand that reaches out to care for those abused, even though that person is quadriplegic and unable to use any of his or her limbs volitionally. By their mere presence in being with the one living in fear, a soul is healed. Or consider the person who is the eye in the body of Christ, yet is considered blind in the world, seeing with 20/20 vision the poverty of the heart in the life of another person simply by listening deeply to another person's story or reading their story in Braille (1 Cor. 12:14–26). Each person is invaluable, with a gift activated within a member of the body by the Spirit, for the common good of all.

Toward Inclusiveness

A congregation or parish that wants to be inclusive of *all* needs to heed the aphorism about "not judging a book by its cover." We all need new ways and new approaches to understanding the various modes of communication that may be used in order for people to exercise their God-given gifts, talents, and services. This will involve giving people plenty of room and support to unveil the gift in themselves, especially in the lives of people the world calls disabled but whom God perceives as a son or daughter of God.

For many people with disabilities, this will be an arduous task because many have been told that they bring nothing of value and worth to the life of a congregation or parish. After all, stories still abound of families with children with disabilities being told not to come to church. Individuals with disabilities are still being shunned simply because they are perceived to be disabled by a church that is unable to appreciate the gift, the talent, and the service that we *all* bring to the body of Christ.

This is where a person with a disability and his or her family and friends almost serve the role and function of a prophet or are prophetic: Sometimes, simply being in the midst of a faith community and struggling to be understood and known as one who is created in the image of God, or being rejected by a faith community simply because of one's disability, is almost prophetic. If a person with a disability is rejected by a faith community simply because of his or her disability, are they not revealing the heart of a congregation, much like prophets revealed the hearts of other people of faith?

Likewise, it will be in other acts of ministry to others in need that the gifts, talents, and services of compassion, teaching, and exhortation will be best known and understood in the community of faith in which they are practiced, by those who are in relationship with, literally, "members, one of another" (Rom. 12). Every person, regardless of what others may think they can or cannot do, is given a gift by the Spirit for the common good of the body of Christ. Having said that, we have not yet answered how this gift is to be understood and utilized in the greater good of the body of Christ. In other words, how does the body work together in order to bring harmony inside the body, for the entire world to see, hear, feel, touch, and taste? This is the focus for the next chapter.

Notes

1. Jean Vanier, *Community and Growth* (Mahwah: Paulist Press, 1979), 23.

2. Walter Brueggemann mentions in some of the lectures and sermons I've heard him preach over the years, that the "Creator creates creation . . . Creation doesn't create the Creator."

3. Brett Webb-Mitchell, *Unexpected Guest at God's Banquet* (New York: Crossroad, 1994). The book has been re-issued recently with Wipf and Stickler, but with a different yet beautiful, meaningful cover.

4. By creative arts, I include a laundry list of ways of being creative, be it woodwork, metal sculpture, computer art, visual art, dance, drama, standup comedy, a sermon, music, laser beam shows, pottery, jewelry, writing plays, composing operas, building sets and scenes, dress making, cooking, building a house, interior design, painting miniature soldiers, singing, clog dancing, two-step, and the list goes on.

5. John Howard Yoder, *The Body Politics* (Nashville: Discipleship Resources, 1992), 51.

6. Anthony Meisel & M. L. del Mastro, *The Rule of St. Benedict* (New York: Image Book, 1975), Ch. 7.

7. Yoder, 50.

8. Yoder, 60.

9. In part two there will be a discussion of discernment. For too long, many people with disabilities have been shunned and ignored in terms of discovering their abilities, gifts, and talents, because the focus was on what a person could *not* do, not on *who* a person is in the body of Christ.

CHAPTER FOUR

Moving toward Community

*On the contrary, the members of the body that seem to
be weaker are indispensable . . . So that there may be
no dissension within the body, but the members may have
the same care for one another.* —1 CORINTHIANS 12:22, 25

*Every Christian community must realize that not only
do the weak need the strong, but also that the strong
cannot exist without the weak. The elimination of the
weak is the death of fellowship.* —DIETRICH BONHOEFFER[1]

The Governor and the Pope

In the previous chapters, the focus was on the nature of the body of
Christ, exploring the contours of this living, breathing, dynamic presence, embodied in those who are part of a church or faith community,
and the importance of realizing that there are gifts, talents, and services instilled in each and every member of our holy gatherings. But what
can a community of faith look, sound, feel, and move like when *all*
members are given a way to be who God created them to be?

Consider this story about the life of the current Governor of New York,
David Paterson:[2] Early on in David Paterson's tenure as Governor of New
York, there was an insightful and amazing article on the life of the new
governor. The article offered a fascinating window into the life of a full-
time politician who is even more interesting and incredible because of the
way he made his way around his world as a man who is legally blind.
And as we have all come to appreciate since he was named governor of
New York, Paterson is a politician regardless of whether he can see.

Governor Paterson became blind when he was a baby because of a condition known as optic atrophy, which damages the optic nerve. His parents decided not to send him to school in New York City, where teachers could not promise that he would be able to interact with students who were not blind. Instead, they sent him to school on Long Island, where he received special attention but also learned alongside students who were not disabled.

His ability to be a fully functioning, fully participating and active, hands-on governor comes not only from his ability to interact and engage with his world, but also from the community of people who make up his world, be it his family members, friends, or his staff. For example:

- He has a phalanx of assistants and a press secretary who, knowing his abilities and limitations, can help him get around a strange room. In eating, he puts a pinch of salt and pepper into the palm of his hand to know how much spice he is spreading. The staff also knows when he is low on fluids and will ask if he needs a refill;

- Rather than being able to read a speech or preach a sermon from a prepared manuscript as I can, he memorizes a speech before delivering it.

- Given all the material that he has to respond to, Governor Paterson listens to long articles or books on a special tape recorder for people who are blind. But he listens to it at a faster speed than usual: "You get used to listening to that Alvin and the Chipmunks voice," he said, referring to the cartoon characters whose speech pattern is higher and faster than ordinary speech patterns.

- He keeps everything in his office and home in the same place in order to move around the rooms easily;

- His reliance on hearing has helped him sharpen a talent useful in politics: an ability to focus on people in a way that makes them feel that they are truly being heard. His attentiveness to people's voices has other political benefits, too: "He can pick up a phony faster than somebody who has sight," said one Assemblyman;

- When he jogs through his former neighborhood in Guilderland, near Albany, he runs the same route each time, every day.

Governor Paterson describes how he understands his place in the world this way: "The secret is how to adjust," he said. "I ask myself how am I going to fit into this world, and how am I going to do it without killing myself?" Although Gov. Paterson often says he does not want people to go out of their way for him, he says society should recognize that he and other people who are blind can't do everything on their own. As one of this first acts as governor, he added instructions to his official state website on how to enlarge the type on the screen. "It's just being more sensitive to people who feel that government and institutions ignore them," he said.

The lesson from Governor Paterson's story is what inclusion looks, sounds, and feels like from his vantage point. And ever since his unexpected rise from lieutenant governor to governor, we also know how mortal, how normal, how ordinary, he is in real life—like all politicians. Sadly, I know that if David Paterson were *not* governor, there would be little or no attempt to make it possible for David Paterson to have all the advantages he currently enjoys. Nevertheless, he is truly "making it" in this world as a political leader on the national stage who just happens to be blind. As for the future? It seems clear that whether or not he wins re-election, as a political leader on the national stage, there will be no campaign issues about his being blind.

A Papal Visit

Contrast this story of Governor Paterson, in which he is an active participant in his life and his destiny, with the visit of Pope Benedict XVI to New York City. For a very brief period of time on a Saturday afternoon, before he addressed a huge throng of young people and seminarians who were outside at St. John's University's large football arena, I watched on television as the Pope visited with several young people with disabilities inside a small chapel at the university. Though this event didn't seem to be as well publicized by the media as his meeting with the larger throngs outside, this quick, fifteen or twenty minute meeting was interesting because of the people who had been gathered together. To attend this meeting, one had to be disabled—or a parent, family member, priest, or religious member who worked with someone with a disability. As he slowly strolled down the central aisle of the chapel's sanctuary, the Pope touched the faces, heads, hands, arms, and legs of young people with various disabling conditions. From a quick look-see, the young people (from elementary school age to people in their twenties) had a variety of disabilities: cerebral palsy, developmental disabilities, blindness and deafness Some children were in wheelchairs and a choir—using sign language—sang a hymn of praise, much to the Pope's delight. The Pope touched the hands of young girls with disabilities as they brought him a gift. No Mass was said with these young people, nor was there time for a simple evening prayer. They simply had a brief time with the Pope.

Segregation or Inclusion?

These two stories present two very different views of people with disabilities: one shows a gentleman with a disability who is leading the state of New York, trying to take control of his environment and community, and making decisions that will affect not only him but many New Yorkers. Paterson thrives in an environment of people who are both able-bodied and disabled because of the spunk and forward thinking of his parents, the supportive community that surrounds him, and his own sense of self-respect and ability. Paterson does not simply "survive" life, but thrives in the life he lives. Paterson's story shows someone with self-respect and ability to live among equals.

In contrast, there is the story of the Pope's visit to New York and the image of the young people with disabilities in submissive postures, who were not even included in and among the throng of well-wishers in the stadium outside. While an argument could be made that this was a special audience with the Pope—audiences are rare—nevertheless the question that comes to the forefront is this: was a person granted an audience with the Pope *solely* because of their disability? If so, was the person with a disability being treated as an object of charity, rather than as a subject of equal worth in God's purview? This story felt more like a throwback to a way of being in the world that is "separate but equal," an approach that did not work in terms of race and—as was reported in the Introduction—has been replaced in educational practices in public schools. I am aware that many communities of faith still gravitate toward a "separate but equal" approach to educating people in the faith, even though this is considered passé in most modern educational circles. Some faith communities invite a respected guardian, assistant, or "reasonable accommodation" person to be present with a person with a disability so that the person with a disability can have access to an educational program, fellowship activity, worship service, young group program, or service project. But it still begs the question: what will true inclusion—rather than mere access—look, feel, and sound like, in which a person with any kind of disability will be fully included and not set aside as a special project, or singled out as a special privilege, simply because of his or her "disabling condition"? What these two very different images have in common is this: a community surrounded both the governor who is blind and the group of young people with disabilities. It is not like they were free-floating individuals; they were persons who were surrounded by a community of caring, concerned members who made a difference in their lives. But the contrast between how the governor and the children with disabilities were treated respectively is remarkable. My hunch is that the governor met with the Pope during his visit in New York in a different context, the two meeting as political leaders, even though they represent different political bodies. The image left by the governor suggests a way of successfully being in the world, regardless of physical ability or limitation. In contrast, there is the image of the submissive children who met with the Pope in a separate, rarefied context solely *because* of their disabilities.

This chapter emphasizes that people with disabilities are to be not only welcomed and accepted into the body of Christ, but *are integral* to the well-being of the body of Christ as equals, not only in God's purview, but in the perspective of the membership of the body of Christ. The primary biblical text for this argument is 1 Corinthians 12:12–31, where Paul highlights the uniqueness of a body that has individual members who have their own remarkable gift to bestow upon others for the greater good of the body of Christ. This gift is as important as any gift given by the Spirit to a person who is non-disabled, whether that person is straight, African-American, female, rich, or lives in Hawaii.

Living Together in the Body of Christ

In this section, we focus on how we are to live, work, worship, pray, serve, and be in fellowship with each other, even as different members of the body. Our "differences" here are not found in our abilities or limitations, or in our disabilities as those are measured by the world around us. Rather, each person plays a specific role and function within the body that they are uniquely gifted, by God's grace, to perform. The trick is discovering or discerning the role and function, gift or service that each person may best contribute to the body of Christ.[3]

In the passages from 1 Cor. 12:14–21, there is a discussion of the order within the organism known as the body of Christ. The foot might regard itself as a lowly member of Christ's body since it carries the weight of the body and gets soiled by walking on the ground. The hand in turn may see itself as being the most effective agent of work, having the primary job of expressing bodily gestures. The eye? It provides vision, considered by most people as a necessary sensory skill, as is the ear's function of hearing.

Which one is more important? None of them or all of them, for they all play an important role in the following ways: first, each is vital and irreplaceable; second, they process and exercise their own duty with dignity within the body of Christ; and third, they can only function fully when they understand that they are bound to the other members who make up the one body that is Christ. Finally, each member can be impeded or limited, through no fault of their own, when another part of the body suffers. Like a spider's web, if you touch one strand of a web, the other strands sense movement and are effected by a simple but new movement; so too if one person experiences a limitation or impediment in being able to fully function within the body, the entire body senses such a possible movement and moment.

It is significant to remember that each part of the body is animated by the Spirit, who alone graces us with the gift that we contribute to the body. And it is the Spirit that decides what part we can play. Here is what is most interesting: since each person plays a part in the body of Christ, as determined by God, then some people will play a role we did not think, well, possible. For example: Gov. Paterson, although legally blind, is figuratively able to see deep into the heart of another person, "spotting" a phony when they speak, as we noted earlier. Likewise, I know people who are deaf or hearing impaired but who have an amazing ability to truly hear what someone is trying to communicate, either by lip reading, reading American Sign Language, or reading a narrative. They understand and hear the other person better than a person who literally has hearing. In other words, even though a person may literally be missing an arm, the use of legs, a foot, an ear, a nose, a mouth, or an eye, that does not preclude them from being able to function figuratively in the body of Christ as an arm, leg, foot, ear, nose, mouth or eye according to how we understand those limbs functioning in the body of Christ. A person in a wheelchair who does not have the ability to walk can still "bring" the Good News to the masses through preaching or some other form of art. The person who is visually impaired, and whose other senses may thus be sharper than others who can see, may see the fragile heart of a parishioner in a crisis by listening to the person's story intently. The person who does not have the ability to smell literally can smell out a person who is not telling the truth, whose moral compass is not working properly, simply by hearing that person's tale, the inflection in the voice, or the constant blinking of eyes.

Striving to Be and Become a Community

In 1 Cor. 12:18–24, there is a description of the arrangement of the body in which each person is where God chooses us to be. Each part is important, for the eye cannot say to the hand "I have no need of you," nor again the head to the feet," I have no need of you" (verses 20, 21).

In verse 22, there is this interesting line: "On the contrary, the members of the body that seem to be weaker are indispensable, and those members of the body that we think less honorable we cloth with greater honor, and our less respectable members are treated with greater respect . . . but God has so arranged the body, giving the greater honor to the inferior member, that there may be no dissension within the body, but the members may have the same care for one another (vss. 22–25).

I have been to many conferences, workshops, service projects, worship and fellowship opportunities in which the clear message was that people with disabilities are clearly the ones who are "less honorable," "less respectable," or are the "inferior members." Why do we draw a distinction between the value of the able-bodied and disabled so quickly? Because in our modern society, people with disabilities today— as was true in and among the people of Israel and the early church no doubt—are treated as less honorable, respectable, and thus inferior, because they are perceived as "broken" and not fully functioning.

But what is interesting is Paul does not write this at all. Instead, we succumb to this interpretation in our reading of 1 Corinthians 12 out of our modern societal context, and our experience of life in faith communities. For many years I have talked about and argued this point: who isn't to say that a person who is less respected is the businessperson who is "morally delayed," or the ethicist who is "ethically challenged"? Perhaps the least respectable or inferior member may be the con man or woman who created a Ponzi scheme, losing billions of dollars of other people's investments through chicanery? Nowhere in our reading of this section should a person with a disability read that she or he is the weaker, less respectable, or inferior member. Yet like all others in the body of Christ, we all sin and fall short of the glory of God (Romans 3:23–24), and the person who is morally bankrupt and ethically inferior is also able to be saved by the salvific grace of God. In contrast to separating and judging people as inferior according to the way the world perceives their respective value, Paul considers the mutuality or egalitarianism of the body of Christ, in which there is an order and sequencing among the many members. In the biblical world, where the apple cart is turned upside down, Paul is showing a paradox in which the less-respectable members of the body are treated with greater respect in the body of Christ. This may be a case of the foolish shaming the wise. The parts of the body of Christ that are highlighted or valued at any given moment differ according to fluid circumstances. The body of Christ needs to be flexible enough in using its members to respond quickly yet with wisdom and compassion to the matters of the overall health of the community of Christ's people.[4]

Understanding how we are to function well within the body of Christ, regardless of who we think we are in the body, above all requires knowing the mind of Christ. Christ is the mind of the body. After all, it is Christ who emptied himself and took on the form of a servant (Phil. 2). It was Christ who not only spoke of God's gift of love, but also is the very embodiment of God's love for the world. The head of the Church—literally and figuratively—is Christ. That is the hierarchy within the body: Christ is the head and the seat of authority over the entire body. And our task is to discern and grow into a deeper knowledge of Christ's will. The head joins and knits together every ligament in the body. What is in the body of Christ is the one promoted "who is the head, from whom the whole body is joined and knit together by every ligament with which it is equipped, as each part is working properly, promoting the body's growth in building itself up in love" (Eph. 4:15, 16).

The body's leadership is not of human origin per se, as is the case of other social groupings and political bodies in which our place is decided by natural kinship structures, modern employment practices, or democratic elections. Within the body of Christ, there is a new "body politic." Rather than separating the valuable from the less valuable, the new politic is this: our place is determined by the gift of the Spirit. Our place is equal in worth, value, respect, and honor, to each and every other part of the body of Christ, regardless if the world calls us "able-bodied" or "disabled." In Christ's body, none of us is disabled, for we are tied into and are integral to the other parts of the body tied into the mind of Christ who—in the name of Christ and in our name—act, function, and play a vital role in the body.[5]

A Still More Excellent Way

Close at hand, there are glimpses of the inclusive community suggested by the metaphor of a body of equal members. At the local YMCA, where I work out almost every night between 6:00 P.M. and 8:00 P.M., I am surrounded by members of a group home who come and work out at around the same time. Beyond the members of the group home, there are other women and men who are visibly disabled . . . well, sort of "disabled." It is in this context that the term "disability" takes on a whole new meaning, if "dis-ability" points to what a body can or cannot do.

For example, I am on the treadmill, running at a good pace. Next to me is a friend who is in her forties and struggling to breathe, and yet modern society would not necessarily call her "disabled," but just "slow" or "struggling." Yet on the other side of me, there is a young man with Down syndrome who proudly wears his t-shirt from the Special Olympics who runs on the treadmill at a clip that is slightly faster than my pace, and yet he is the one considered "dis-abled." Obviously, his body is fine and he is quite able to run.

Likewise, I am in the fitness area, lifting weights and pulling on cables while another young man with cerebral palsy is next to me. He is struggling to control the movement of hands, arms, torso, and head as the cerebral palsy that he lives with tries to thwart his ability to manage the heavy weight over and around his body. But the young man is tenacious, grunting, groaning, and expressing a loud "tsk" as he pushes the bar with weights over his head. He does not ask for help, nor take it from me when I ask him "do you want a spot?" "Nah," he responds simply, between gasps for air.

In 1 Cor. 12: 25, 26, we are called to have empathy with each other in the body of Christ, having the same care for one another, in which if one suffers we all suffer together; and if one member is honored, we all rejoice together. As the members of the YMCA, who happen to be disabled, look out for the needs of other people first rather than necessarily thinking of themselves, we—the able-bodied—are to practice the same empathetic response. As members of the Church body, we are to let go of petty resentments toward other congregants, make good decisions, and ask God in Christ for help in doing what is right, good, and loving.

When there is conflict in the body, we need to remember that we are not like other organizations in this world, for we have the mind of Christ guiding our actions and behaviors, attitudes and mindsets. As I have read and been taught by the Benedictines, there is this truth: that life without another person is only half a life. While we have to live with one another to have a full life, human imperfection due to sin will still be part of our reality. Joan Chittister reminds us that, in Benedictine spirituality, community is a very human thing: "We do not expect perfection here, but we do expect growth, in ourselves as well as in others"[6]

Crises and conflict are not necessarily bad in and of themselves. Much good can come out of a crisis, for it can be a time of discovering the good we share in common, as well as those things that we do not share. Crisis confronted and aired, which is given time to be processed, can, in the end, make a community stronger as people are bonded together with stronger friendships that incorporate tension as a creative part of a relationship.[7]

There is a movie that captures well a community that moves from the status quo, through crisis and conflict, to an unexpected place and time of inclusion of *all* its members, *Lars and the Real Girl*.[8] The main character of this film, Lars, is a "loner" of sorts, though many in the mental health services could read a lot of symptoms in his life's story. He is, as one reviewer called him, a "holy fool and a martyr in waiting, a subject of mockery and a means of redemption."[9] Set in Anywhere, Midwest America, Lars lives with his brother and sister-in-law, although more accurately he is living behind them in a small, separate house.

Lars's social awkwardness influences his relationship with family, friends, and any possible relationship with women. What breaks him out of his rut is when his co-workers, surfing on the web, discover a site that sells life-size mannequins.. Without anyone knowing it, Lars orders a life-size doll, Bianca, who has large lips and an even larger bust. With Bianca, Lars converses about missionary trips to South America, his ideal American dream, and his desire to be in a serious relationship with another person, namely Bianca. Even though there is a love-interest in Lars's world, a young woman, she can only watch from the sidelines as Lars falls in love with Bianca.

What was most telling about this movie were the scenes in which, with the introduction of Bianca into their midst, the entire Midwestern town transforms itself from a straight-laced, average, normal town of folk, into a caring community of friends. There is a meeting of Lars's family and friends, including a minister of the local church, who deliberate about how to handle this new presence in the town. With no real leadership per se, except for some outspoken, caring individuals, the decision is to care for Lars unconditionally, no questions asked, and to treat Bianca as if she were "one of them." What unfolds is a group of town folk who take Bianca into their lives, with Bianca attending worship, singing hymns, going to public meetings, even to the point of being elected to be on the local school board. Lars is frustrated because Bianca is now going out with others during the weekday nights, and is busier in the affairs of the town than he is. What was beautiful in this film is the way the community included Lars and Bianca, with little in the way of "ifs, ands, or buts." It was moving to see a community include Lars and Bianca in their ordinary lives, treating them as if they were family, even in the context of the Church. The story of Lars and Bianca gives us at least one picture of what an inclusive community may look like.

In the last verse of 1 Corinthians 12:27, after Paul finishes giving us a general overview of the way we are to be the body of Christ with one another, he ends with this line: "But strive for the greater gifts, and I will show you a more excellent way." This passage immediately precedes 1 Corinthians 13:1, which begins with Paul's soliloquy about love. It is love that will, in the end, provide not only the glue, the tendons, the sinews to the body's musculature, but the very energy, zest, and desire to be inclusive of one another in the body of Christ.

Readers will have different ideas about what inclusion—the more excellent way—could look, feel, sound, and smell like and how how it can be achieved in their own churches. Accordingly, part two of this book provides actionable steps for leading a congregation or parish into becoming a fully inclusive community of Christ's people.

Notes

1. Dietrich Bonhoeffer, *Living Together*, (New York: Harper and Row, 1954).

2. Jeremy Peters, "A Blind Governor Adjusts, and So Does Albany" in nyt.com, April 21, 2008.

3. Much of this section comes from a paper I delivered in a conference in Portland, OR, under the title, "Beyond the Ramp: Toward Full Inclusion of People with Disabilities in the Church," May 2008.

4. A deeper discussion of this subject is in my book *Christly Gestures* (Grand Rapids: Eerdmans, 2003), 68.

5. Ibid., 72.

6. Joan Chittister, Wisdom Distilled from the Daily (San Francisco: Harper One, 1991), p 47.

7. Webb-Mitchell, *Christly Gestures*, 83.

8. Craig Gillespie, dir., *Lars and the Real Girl* (Actors: Ryan Gosling, Patricia Clarkson, Emily Mortimer, Paul Schneider). Produced by Sidney Kimmel, John Cameron, Sarah Aubrey, Studio: MGM, 2007.

9. Manohla Dargis, "A Lonely Guy Plays House with a Mail Order Sex Doll." see www.nyt.com (accessed October 12, 2007).

PART TWO

From Acceptance to Full Inclusion: The Practice

*We have gifts that differ according
to the grace given to us.* —ROMANS 12:6

*For "Let everyone that comes be received as Christ,"
that most familiar phrase of the Rule of St. Benedict, at once
says that hospitality means more than simply the open door,
and the place at table: it means warmth, acceptance,
enjoyment in welcoming whoever has arrived.*
—ESTHER DE WAAL[1]

Within the Church, the body of Christ, the move toward full inclusion and equal participation of people with disabilities will not be automatic or easy. There is not a one-size-fits-all approach or method for being a fully-inclusive faith community. For many, if not most congregations and parishes, working toward such a state of being will be unprecedented, because it calls upon each person in a gathering of believers to be honestly and forthrightly who they are, right where they are, "warts and all" as some would say. Typically, we place safeguards to protect us from being too "messy" while in the presence, sight, or range of hearing of others, especially when coming to worship God. As a consequence, honesty may require a new book of etiquette and manners in how we live open lives as members of Christ's body. Even though the Holy Spirit is fully aware of our nature, as are we all when we are quiet and reflective or caught in a crisis situation, that is not how we like to present ourselves to the world. Yet such genuineness is key and elemental to being a fully inclusive body, where vulnerability, intimacy, and love may thrive.

Both people with disabilities and those who are able-bodied will find being fully inclusive—which can only occur when we are fully vulnerable with one another and thus trusting of one another in the body of Christ—a noble long term strategy, but one that they would prefer not to seek. After all, even with the passage of the Americans with Disabilities Act in 1990, and all the official Church polity statements that were made in the last half of the previous century in support of full inclusion of people with disabilities in faith communities—alongside all of the conferences, workshops, books (like this one), and movie/video witnesses affirming the place and presence of people with disabilities in congregations and parishes—there is simply a trickle, if that, of people with disabilities discovering or responding to the invitation to come and be a full participant of and in a community of faith, let alone discovering their place and presence in the body.

Part two describes the actionable steps and strategies for working toward full inclusion of *all* who desire to participate more fully in communities of faith where work is shared among the members of a congregation or parish who are able-bodied *and* the so-called community of people with disabilities.[2] To anticipate the chapters that follow, for a congregation or parish to be more inclusive, it will need to focus on: 1) welcome or hospitality; 2) acceptance and accessibility; 3) inclusion as co-creation; and 4) the practice of love. These actions need to occur simultaneously or with some level of synchronicity. I am breaking the overall process into parts to help congregations and parishes work through each step separately toward being inclusive. Chapter four covers the practice of welcome, of hospitality. This seems a necessary "first move" toward full inclusion. This is because many people with disabilities are still simply not welcomed into many churches by pastors, priests, lay leaders, religious educators, choir directors, church musicians, youth leaders, and others. Likewise, there are people with disabilities who, because of being ostracized by many faith communities, find it hard to welcome those who are non-disabled into their lives. This first move is asking the question: "What do we do when there is a stranger at the threshold of the doors leading into and out of the church?" Where we enter and leave from symbolizes our comings and goings throughout the seasons of our lives. This is why the first move is welcoming.[3]

Chapter five discusses accessibility and acceptance in such a way that the two terms seem intertwined with one another. For example, physically or architecturally, some churches are not accessible, and find it difficult to move toward fuller accessibility as a result. In these instances, we would say that such a structure reflects the heart of a congregation that is not very accepting of people with disabilities. In a church where I once served as interim pastor, there was an outcry by some members of the church when the pews in the front of the sanctuary were shortened to provide a place for people in wheelchairs. Other congregants and parishioners find it difficult to alter the front of a church with ramps or lifts for people in wheelchairs or who are using walkers. Still others complain about the large movie screens in a sanctuary, where the words of a hymn or a prayer are projected, even though it is easier for people who are visually impaired to read. But this is about more than the issue of physical or architectural accessibility. It is about programmatic accessibility, let alone accessibility *and* acceptance into each other's hearts, minds, and physical embrace.

Chapter six explores the pathway of full participation and inclusion, by considering carefully and intentionally the co-creative process between and among members of a faith community. Co-creation looks at the process of making something anew between two or more people, as it takes a community to make or create something. As mentioned earlier, no one is truly sui generis. To paraphrase the African-American proverb, it takes a village to create something, and to be creative. This is because we take our ideas of what we are going to create from the environment, the context, and the relationships that we are or are not a part of in our daily lives. Because some people with disabilities are not capable of processing and/or communicating as easily as others, the co-creative/co-creation process will take more time, effort, and concentration, as well as a commitment of a community that is intent on letting one and all within a community of faith express their ideas, thoughts, and feelings. Full inclusion and participation will be reached within a community of faith when one and all are able to first, respond to the call that draws out one's gifts, talents, and services, and second, the gifts, talents, and services are not only utilized, but nurtured and enhanced within and among the members of the body of Christ. It is then that the gifts that are given to us all—each and every one, as deigned by the Creator God—will be fully realized in the context of the body of Christ.

The final chapter, the Conclusion, is on the practice of love. Esther de Waal writes prophetically that "love, trust, acceptance—these are things that I receive from Christ, and it is only as I come to know and to love Christ and to realize that I am known and loved, that I can also love my fellows."[4] What is the source of welcoming, acceptance, accessibility, justice, and inclusion of all *but* the love of God in Christ for each and every one of us, regardless of whatever category or label society might slap upon us.

Notes

1. Esther de Waal, *Seeking God: The Way of St. Benedict* (Collegeville: Liturgical Press, 1984), 120.

2. Again, I use "so-called community" language because of the very heterogeneity found in and among gatherings of people with disabilities. There is diver-

sity among the various kinds of disabilities and ways of being disabled. But there is also the issue of intersecting identities, in which a person is more than her or his disability. With intersecting identities, we are presented with multiple opportunities to relate to and be in solidarity with people on manifold issues, be it one's ethnicity, nationality, gender, sexual orientation, age, economic class, educational background . . . and the list goes on.

3. See Martin Marty and Micah Marty in *When True Simplicity is Gained: Finding Spiritual Clarity in a Complex World* (Grand Rapids: Eerdmans, 1998).

4. Esther de Waal, 124.

CHAPTER FIVE

Hospitality and the Stranger

I was hungry and you gave me food,
I was thirsty and you gave me something to drink,
I was a stranger and you welcomed me. —MATTHEW 25:35

All guests to the monastery should be welcomed as Christ,
Because He will say, "I was a stranger,
and you took me in." —THE RULE OF ST. BENEDICT

To welcome is not primarily to open the doors of our house.
It is to open the doors of our heart and become vulnerable.
It is a spirit, an inner attitude. —JEAN VANIER[1]

Welcoming Jesus: A Missed Opportunity?

In the previous section, I proposed that each and everyone of us is not only created in the image of God, making us relational and creative beings, but that we are given gifts and talents, and are called to serve one another in the body of Christ. Jean Vanier of l'Arche concurs: "If we really welcome each new person as a gift of God, as His messenger, we would be more loving and more open."[2] That is why each and every new welcome is very important because either it makes someone feel like they are treasured as a human being, or like they are not welcome to be part of a gathering.

The importance of how a community welcomes each other and practices[3] hospitality was underlined for me in one of my initial visits to l'Arche.[4] In 1984, my former wife and I made our first visit to the l'Arche community in Lambeth, England, just outside of London proper. L'Arche is an internationally renowned religious community for and with people, primarily adults, with developmental disabilities. Upon arriving at the community, a lovely tradition caught me and my former wife off guard. On our bedside table, in the room in which we were staying, there was a lovely small bouquet of flowers. The beauty of this simple bouquet, this sign of welcome, was to find out that the flowers were collected by one of the residents or core members of the community, an older woman with a developmental disability, and not one of the assistants.

After living, working, playing, and researching the l'Arche community, I came to appreciate in time how it was often the person who was living with a disability who extended hospitality to strangers like us, rather than some of the presumably able-bodied assistants. From making a cup of tea on the spur of the moment for a party of two or more to collecting flowers for another visitor, from taking out the trash to answering phone calls and knocks on the door with a pleasant voice, from preparing a meal to preparing a table for a meal, the simple acts of the residents signaled a genuine welcome.

One act of welcome I remember with a certain sad fondness. When I took a group of undergraduates to live in this community, one of the older women of the community, Rosie—a cantankerous woman—was a collector of mugs. She went to the nearest five-and-dime store adjacent to the community and collected cheap porcelain, mass produced mugs, some decorated with flowers, others with butterflies, and one or two with the image of the Royal Family. One of my students, when given a mug by Rosie, politely gave the mug back to her, causing a great heartache in Rosie. Rosie cried because it was not the mug that was rejected, but the offer she personally made to be a gift-giver. *She* felt rejected by the young student.

What my student failed to appreciate was the gift of hospitality, of welcome, being extended to him by Rosie. Afterward, when talking to the young student, he clearly understood Rosie to be one of the "least of these" of Jesus' extended family or household, rather than seeing himself as the stranger referred to in the Matthew passage. But the young student's response left him—and me—questioning if he was not the one who was the "least of these." The question at the end of the day was this: did both Rosie and the student miss an opportunity to welcome Jesus into their lives?

What I've discovered time and again in working, worshiping, playing, learning, and being with people with disabilities is the possibility of conversion. Welcoming and being in the presence of people who are not necessarily like me—white, Anglo-Saxon, Protestant, well-educated, and gay—I've learned to be the stranger and likewise to welcome the stranger in my midst. I've learned that when I am the stranger in the crowd, much like Rosie, or am in the presence of the stranger who is not like me or our folks, I invite the possibility of welcoming angels unawares (Hebrews 13:2), and the possibility of conversion: being and becoming more like Christ, participating more willingly in what some call the Jesus-life.[5] All this from the simple act of welcoming, of hospitality!

Make Way for the Image of God!

Richard Rohr argues that it is the outcast—the poor, the little ones who come before the Church, the insecure, and those with disability or addiction—who brings us the questions on the edge of life, showing us in turn what are the real issues. By confronting us with these questions, the poor dispel our illusions about what is normative, and likewise raise the additional questions: what does it mean to be a Christian and an active participant in the body of Christ?[6]

Because worship of God is central to our existence as members of the body of Christ, one of the places where I am surprised again and again to discover the difference between what I consider to be normal and what is of God—they are not usually the same—is in worship with people with disabilities. After I have worshipped with people with disabilities, I am always thankful for the wake-up call. That is why I am a big advocate of inclusive worship on Sunday morning at the "main hour" for worship, which today is either 10 A.M. or 11 A.M. Again, while this hour has become the most segregated hour in the Christian Church, separating people based on race, class, age, gender, sexual orientation, and nationality—to name just a few of the cultural labels—it is also one of the primary places in which inclusion must first take place. How a church performs the sacred act and ritual of worship reflects the abiding ethos or ethic of a people gathered in prayer, fellowship, and service. As I've argued in my other books, worship is a "school of Christian education," where the members of the body are being formed and nurtured as they go back out into the world on their daily pilgrimage. If our worship of God is inclusive, then the other programs and activities in the life of a congregation will be so too. People will say to themselves,

"Well, we worship together! I guess we can visit, learn, pray, and serve with one another as well."

Sadly, genuinely inclusive worship services in which everyone is welcomed are not yet common. Even before the worship service begins, I am amazed at the unevenness of how strangers are or are not welcomed into a church building, especially people with disabilities. Again and again, I hear of stories that people with disabilities—and their family, friends, and advocates—are politely discouraged from coming back to a church at the conclusion of worship with the words from a pastor, "I don't think we're the best church for your family. Try another church next Sunday!" In the midst of worship, there are occasions where I have watched choirs of able-bodied teenagers perform a song in sign language, but was aware that there was no one signing or in a congregation who was deaf or used sign language on a regular basis. Or I attended some of the most progressive churches in my area, after they had rebuilt their sanctuary, noticing still how many steps were used to get in and around the worship space with no ramps whatsoever. We have much to learn about how to welcome the stranger to our midst. Yet, in contrast, I've also attended worship in churches where the crucifer or cross bearer is a young woman living with Down syndrome, or the young man leading us in prayer is doing so with a voice-activated device that gives voice to the words that he has carefully typed. I am amazed at how large Bibles printed in Braille are, and even more amazed at watching someone read the lectionary using that very same Bible. It is at times like this that I remember my friend and former colleague at Duke Divinity School, John Westerhoff, remarking that we should be shouting at moments like this, "Make way for the Image of God! The Imago Dei comes forth!" For we are all created in the image of God.

Welcoming the Stranger: Recovering the Lost Art of Hospitality

In terms of people with disabilities, many churches either have never learned or have forgotten the art or practice of welcome and how to include people with disabilities into their midst. Many churches reflect the missed opportunity of welcoming Jesus. And for churches that do try to welcome people with disabilities, most are at the starting gate, or what baseball aficionados would call the "first base," of learning to welcome people with disabilities. This is, after all, the first and most crucial move: being welcoming or acting hospitable to and with people with disabilities.

I fully understand that I am writing this book out of this basic assumption: most congregations and parishes do not understand that they are a gathering of either "sin sick souls" or people who themselves are "standing in the need of prayer," as the words of the hymn express it. In many congregations there is a sense that "all is well," except for the few on our prayer lists. Meanwhile, there is an almost natural drive within a congregation or parish to welcome primarily people who are more like us than different. Being "like us" means sharing the same ethnicity, national heritage, skin color, political and theological affiliation, economic status, or intellectual breadth. The tendency to welcome those who are like us also exists in churches comprised primarily of people with some disabilities, such as those serving the deaf or hearing impaired.

Yet repeatedly, I find evidence that people in our congregations are more like the disabled than they might suppose. In the course of presenting many workshops, sermons, and papers on the topic of the place and presence of people with disabilities in faith communities, I am always surprised by how many people respond negatively to the question, "Does anyone here have a disability?" Folks do not raise a hand, stand, or raise their voice to indicate that they have a disability, even though the majority of us—this writer included—have eyesight problems. We simply fail to recognize that many of us are living, by and large, with a visual disability needing corrective eyewear or surgery. I believe that Lens Crafters and other eyewear companies have been so successful in "selling" their glasses as a fashion accessory that the thought of eyewear as a disability is not on a lot of people's radar.

Furthermore, as people age, a slightly smaller group of people will find themselves living with a hearing disorder, while still others will sooner or later live with an invisible disability like diabetes, a heart condition, cancer, Alzheimer's, or some other malady. While most visual disabilities and hearing disabilities are considered "normative" for an ageing population, these other conditions are not understood as a disability per se. These otherwise invisible or hidden disabilities are simply not discussed, but are considered a "private matter" among families. And some times, living with a mental illness, such as clinical depression or a bi-polar disorder, is not considered a disability but as something that we do not need to talk about.

There are a plethora of reasons for explaining why congregations and parishes, even among the religious leaders, are slow to admit that someone is living with a disability. For example when I taught courses at Duke Divinity School and would press the issue of disability concerns in my classes, many of my students would simply yawn from boredom because they were living in a world in which a disability was not part of who they are. Years later, after they themselves came down with a disability, or family members did, they would soon be in touch with me to ask about references and resources. Others simply do not want to consider how fragile life is, thus keeping people with obvious disabilities at arms length. For many people who are non-disabled, a person with a disability represents a "fate worse than death" said one parishioner to me after discussions on being an inclusive congregation.

Yet there is also this phenomenon: creating a faith community ghetto or gulag for people with disabilities. There are specific ministries *for* people *with* disabilities in and among Christian communities of faith. There are churches created by well-meaning pastors who took people with severe or profound disabilities out of mainline churches for "special worship services" on Sunday morning at an alternative place of worship. There are also mainline churches that have set aside a "special time of worship" on Sunday nights or some other day of the week for people who are severely or profoundly intellectually challenged, based on the assumption that people with disabilities would not understand what is going on during worship with people who are largely non-disabled. Rather than challenge the presumptions of worship—that only those "like us" with a certain intelligent quotient or appropriate social adaptation behaviors can come and understand worship—these churches have simply segregated worship at the normal ten o'clock or eleven o'clock hour. The sadness is that worship is usually not in our control if it is a place where God in Christ is worshipped. We may set the ritual, the liturgy together, but at a certain point of worship, we as creatures of the Creator can only and must only simply turn our worship over to the God who is forever challenging our assumptions and the behaviors that embody those assumptions. As Annie Dillard has written in one of her books, before we worship God we should dole out crash helmets and snap seat belts in the pew because we may awake the sleeping God.[7] Or to quote Frederick Buechner when writing about the mystery of baptism, "When it comes to the forgiving and transforming love of God, one wonders if the six-week-old screecher knows all that much less than the Archbishop of Canterbury."[8] Of course, the same could be said of Eucharist, of prayer. . . indeed, of the entire Sunday morning liturgy. Who of us understand at the deepest levels or parts of our being that has been touched or been confronted until long after worship is over?

In this chapter, the stress is on learning the first move, the first step, the first action of being and becoming a more inclusive congregation that is welcoming or hospitable to people whom the world calls "disabled." It is also the first step for a community or gathering of people with disabilities, even in a larger church organization comprised primarily of people with disabilities, like a church of people who are deaf. There is an art to learning the practice of hospitality, especially with those who consider people with disabilities to be outsiders and strangers. For most churches that are populated by people who are non-disabled, the person who is disabled and coming into our midst is often considered to be a stranger, sometimes simply the "Other," in our community life. And it is in the stranger, the Other who doesn't play our games, that we discover not only the hidden and hated parts of our own souls, but the Lord Jesus Christ himself. In welcoming the stranger, we make room for the Other, for God. As Richard Rohr writes, that is why the Church is always converted when the outcasts and those on the margins—those whom we shunted aside because they are not like us, like people with disabilities—are reinvited into the holy gathering. With that invitation, we create the possibility of conversion.[9] The good news is that the stranger when they are welcomed into the Christian community, when they take a front and center space in worship, may change our communities for the better by teaching us how to live the Gospel.

There are many examples to follow in learning to be a welcoming community to people with disabilities. One of the best examples is the Benedictine community, though in all honesty and modesty, Benedictine communities are always learning and re-learning this simple and essential practice. In the Rule of St. Benedict, the Benedictine communities are instructed to engage in an essential practice: welcoming strangers, for they are Christ. When one first comes into the community, Benedictines are called to show "every courtesy, especially to servants of

God and pilgrims." A superior, brother, or sister greets the stranger with charity, and ideally prays with the stranger in order to be at peace. The greeting and farewell of a guest should be offered, "with great humility for with bowed head and a prostrate body all shall honor in the guests the person of Christ. For it is Christ who is really being received."[10]

The following section explores in more depth the issues at hand in welcoming into our midst the Stranger, who in the case of this book is the one with a disability. After all, welcoming or practicing hospitality is the first move toward becoming a congregation or parish that fully includes people with disabilities.

Practicing Hospitality

What Is Hospitality?

Hospitality means being hospitable, or welcoming and friendly to a guest. In most dictionaries, the word "welcome" is associated and followed-up with the word "guest." In other words, in welcoming, you cannot have "welcome" without "guest."

In her book *Making Room*, Christine Pohl writes that hospitality is a fundamental moral practice for communal life. It is "necessary to human well-being and essential to the protection of vulnerable strangers."[11] Harkening back to the ancient texts, Pohl explores the word hospitality, citing the ancient Greek word for hospitality, *philoxenia*. This word is a combination of the word for love or affection for people who are friends, *philia*, and the word for stranger, *xenos*. Pohl writes that this word for hospitality shows how closely it aligns love with the stranger. "Because *philoxenia* includes the word for stranger, hospitality's orientation toward strangers is also more apparent in Greek than in English."[12] In a sense, hospitality is a combination of love of God and love of neighbor, even when the neighbor is a stranger, since this love—philia—is a practice that we learn from God first loving us.

Threshold into Community

Whether a person with a disability, or his or her family members, are welcomed the first time they visit the church matters, and it is often the main variable in determining whether a person or a group returns.

Where is the first place or area that many of us experience hospitality? In part two's opening narrative, I cited the importance of the threshold or portal gateway, and many who have written on the act or art of hospitality refer to the importance of our response to the person who is at the threshold or gateway into the heart of a community:

> This threshold (of the doors we enter and leave from) comes to stand for the comings and goings of people throughout the days and years ... the threshold prompts us to measure those comings and goings in a new way. Living is simple when the threshold is smooth enough for the innocent to cross and enter our lives and strong enough to bar the beguilers. God rightly frames the door to our souls and our lives as promised, and friend and neighbor freely cross its threshold.[13]

The threshold or portal gateway is both literal—the actual entry way and exit—and figurative when it refers to the portal into our hearts, minds, and bodies in the body of Christ.

Entryways and exits to faith communities—both physical and architectural, as well as the human presence at such entryways—are key to welcoming and extending hospitality to people with disabilities. Here is why: as I mentioned earlier, I have met a lot of families with children with disabilities who were told by pastors or priests of churches they visited for the first time that, while they were glad to have the family with them on Sunday morning for worship, "perhaps you would feel more comfortable in another congregation." The pastor literally shook the hands of the family members while escorting them out of church, simply because they had a child with a disability. This interchange happened on the threshold, at the entry portal of a sanctuary. I have also sat and worked with family members in finding a church home after a pastor or religious leader made it clear that they were not welcome to bring a child with a disability like Attention Deficit Hyperactivity Disorder to a children's sermon because the child acted out inappropriately. I've also been with those who have had an adult member in the family with Alzheimer's walk away during worship, an incident to which the governing church board responded by asking the family to not bring the member with the disability back into their midst. And I've recounted in other books the story of Jill from Massachusetts who lived her life with a mental illness. She was told by a pastor not to attend a certain church anymore because she answered all the questions in the children's sermon, told people loudly how much she put in the offering, and ate most of the doughnuts during fellowship. Yet Jill said no one ever told her not to answer the pastor's questions; she thought she was being helpful in shouting out how much she gave; and no one said there was a limit in how many doughnuts she ate.

A factor that makes the issue of how, when, and why a church welcomes someone with a disability more complex still is this: I've worked with churches in which a person who was raised in a new church and who did not have a disability initially was still accepted as a part of the congregation after the onset of a disability. However, this same congregation could not find it in their hearts to welcome a person with a disability who came from *outside* of the congregation. Simply because one person with a disability is part of a congregation or parish does not mean that others are also welcomed.

One of the questions for the reader is this: is your congregation or parish ready and trained to simply say "Hello, and welcome to our church!" to *all* who wish to come and worship? The responsibility for extending a hearty and genuine welcome usually falls upon the shoulders of ushers, lay, and religious leaders.

Hospitality in Scripture

Christine Pohl argues that hospitality is key to Paul's understanding of being the community of Christ, citing Romans 15:7, in which Paul urges all believers to "welcome one another" as Christ welcomed us.[14] But in Christ welcoming us, what is important to remember is that Jesus, from what we know of his three years of active ministry, never had a home to welcome anyone into. I once heard the late Brother Roger of the Taize community refer to Jesus as the Pilgrim God. Jesus was often in the position of needing others to provide hospitality, like the hospitality provided by Mary, Martha, Lazarus, and Zacheus, to name a few. Even though Jesus did not have a home, he nevertheless practiced hospitality. He fed thousands of women, men, and children; he hosted his disciples with a Passover meal that we, today, call the "Last Supper"; he sat down with the disciples who were on their way to Emmaus; and he fed fishermen a breakfast on a sandy rock-strewn shoreline of the Sea of Galilee. So Jesus set forth an example of hospitality that we are to follow today as one of the gestures of the kingdom or reign of God's love.

Pohl continues by pointing to biblical passages that challenge the body of Christ to be hospitable, like in Romans 12:13, Hebrews 13:2, and 1 Peter 4:9. She writes: "Hospitality, in each of these passages, is a concrete expression of love—love for sisters and brothers, love extended outward to strangers, prisoners, and exiles, love that attends to physical and social needs. Within acts of hospitality, needs are met, but hospitality is truncated if it does not go beyond physical needs . . . it also includes recognizing and valuing the stranger or guest."[15] What hospitality embodies is love. After all, it is one thing to ask the practical questions of accessibility for people with disabilities, such as are the doors wide enough to welcome wheelchairs or other equipment used to help people get in and out of a structure, such as a walker? And once a person with a disability is in, are there Bibles, hymnbooks, or bulletins that are decipherable for *all* to utilize? And if not, are there any other means by which people with disabilities can participate? But it is another thing to simply love a person for who she or he is as someone created in the image of God, regardless of a person's abilities or limitations.

There is one more place in Scripture where hospitality assumes a prominent position: Hospitality has slowly been understood by those with disabilities through the lens of the parable of the Great Banquet Feast, Luke 14:15–24.[16] In this parable, the servant—namely Jesus—welcomes a group of people to come to a great banquet that his master is hosting. All the supposedly able-bodied guests fail to show up. And those who are invited *and* who also attend the gracious banquet? Primarily the outsiders to such events, or people that we would call today disabled. In this parable, the paradigmatic example of the realm or reign of God is established. All people, regardless of what they can or cannot do, have a place at the table because of who and whose they are. This being the case, it follows that the Church, the body of Christ, in which the very "marrow" of the "bones" of the body exhibits the same inclusive design, should be equally welcoming, accepting, and inclusive . . . just as Jesus was in his earthly ministry. For whenever we pray "on earth, as it is in heaven," we pray that we will be more like heaven than not. And that means welcoming people with disabilities, does it not?

Strangers Welcoming Strangers

Christine Pohl writes about the circumstances of the ancient Israelites in what we would call today the Middle East. The Israelites lived a precarious existence, yet they went out of their way to welcome the stranger, the sojourner, just as they had been welcomed as the stranger or the sojourner by God. The protection God provided established a covenant with God which provided a model for integrating the pilgrim into the communal life of Israel.[17] Thus hospitality was associated with God, covenant, and blessing.[18]

What is important about how the pilgrim nation of Israel extended hospitality to strangers is that when we, who are non-disabled, welcome a person with a disability—and his or her family and friends—it is truly stranger meeting stranger. We are both strangers unto one another, never having met each other before. Likewise, it is awkward yet wonderful when those of us who are non-disabled are welcome to come, as strangers, into a gathering or community of believers who also happen to be disabled. In these instances, we may be the strangers.

Yet there is a deeper kind of welcome among strangers that is also occurring, especially among many of those who are non-disabled and have never confronted limitations or inabilities in their lives, let alone their mortality. A friend once told me that the reason he is uncomfortable with people with disabilities is because, in the immediacy of the moment, he realizes that what he is able to do today can all be gone tomorrow, in the blink of an eye because of an accident. That is the "stranger" and the "strangeness" that he experiences and does not wish to welcome into the elaborate high-wire act he has created in what most Americans would call a successful life. The loss of a bodily function, the cessation of sight, the impairment of the thinking process—all cause him great discomfort, and are a part of his life that he would consider a stranger or alien presence. He fears most becoming a stranger unto himself, and the presence of a person with a crutch, a cane, or a wheelchair, is almost more than he can handle. What he fails to understand is what the disability rights activist, the late Harriet McBryde Johnson, understood only too well. That those whose limbs are supported by an iron frame, a crutch, a wheelchair, a prosthetic device or limb: "are athletic elites. They picked up the stuff we hard-core crips dropped."[19] There will be more on confronting and accepting our mortal selves—whether one is considered non-disabled or disabled—in the coming chapter on accessibility and acceptance.

In her book, *An Altar in the World*, Barbara Brown Taylor picks up on the importance of being the stranger ourselves in order to know what it is to welcome the stranger among us. She writes: "You shall love the stranger first of all because you know what it is to be a stranger yourself.

Second of all, you shall love the stranger because the stranger shows you God."[20]

I have preached this very sentiment many times in my life as a Presbyterian pastor. Before we can truly understand what it is to welcome the stranger, we need to first be a stranger somewhere in this life, dependent upon the goodwill of others. As cited above, the young student did not quite understand the art of gift giving in the act of hospitality, probably because he himself had never been a stranger before.

On pilgrimages that I've taken around the world, I have most often been the stranger in an alien land. As a stranger or alien, not understanding the language and often misreading the cultural cues, I was led, as if by the hand, by many who knew their culture well and who could tell me where I should sit, how I should eat the food that was strange to my taste buds, and how to graciously say "thanks," and "no thanks." What is most important in being the stranger is acting with a kind of powerlessness. In other words, for a brief time in our lives, we are not in control but are reliant on the goodwill of others who are more or less in power. Learning to be a gracious guest is an art unto itself.

The principles behind welcoming and being the stranger suggest that church members who are non-disabled, and especially religious leaders, should spend time in a position of powerlessness, of not being in control, and of being dependent or reliant upon others, so that they can better understand how it feels to be powerless and to be a stranger in a strange land. By experiencing a sense of powerlessness, members in a religious community may better anticipate the needs of those who are disabled, and who may be visiting or be interested in joining a faith community. It is in the act of being lost, of being out of power, out of control if you will, that we become better hosts, learning how to be better equipped for assuming the role and function of a host in practicing hospitality and being a welcoming presence for others.

In regard to people with disabilities and faith communities, it is clear that many come into a congregation or parish with little knowledge of the customs of a community. Without delay, it will be important to initiate the person with a disability into the practices that are used in a community's worship of God. But also important, and without losing the main importance of a ritual, the worship needs to be adapted or modified so that it is inclusive of a person with a disability, rather than making a person with a disability make all the accommodations. While the liturgy or framework of worship may be set by denominational bodies, what goes on in and during the worship of God is usually sufficiently flexible to meet the needs of all rather than a select few.

What is most needed in welcoming the stranger is learning to be gracious or grace-filled in our actions. Without reading into or reading ahead of what another person wants or needs, it is important to realize that in the Christian context welcoming a stranger is truly welcoming none other than Christ. Christ may show up in a wheelchair, or he may be that person using a walker or cane. Christ might not be able to read the bulletin's small print, nor turn a Bible's onion pages. Christ might need a magnifying glass for singing hymns, or he may need the words from the hymnal or sermon to be projected on a big screen in the front of the sanctuary.

The Importance of Baptism

People in religious communities may best learn the practice of welcome and hospitality with the sacramental ritual of baptism.[21] While we are created in the image of God, knit together by God in our mother's womb (Ps. 139) and saved by grace through faith (Ephesians 2), baptism is the outward sign and symbol of what God in Christ is doing: receiving us into the body of Christ publicly. In baptism, a person (infant or adult) is welcomed as a stranger into the body of Christ. For example, in the tradition of the Presbyterian Church (USA), the Minister of Word and Sacrament says that "in baptism God claims and seals us to show that we belong to God . . . by water and the Holy Spirit, we are made members of the church, the body of Christ, and joined to Christ's ministry of love and peace and justice." These words are followed by asking the one who is to be baptized and/or his or her family members or guardian a series of questions: "Do you renounce evil and its power in the world, which defy God's righteousness and love? Do you renounce the ways of sin that separate you from the love of God?"[22] After professing the faith with the words of the Apostles' Creed, in the gesture of applying water to another person, there is the Trinitarian invocation as one is baptized in the name of the "Father and of the Son, and of the Holy Spirit."[23] With the gesture of water being poured or sprinkled upon the baptized, there are literally the "words of welcome," in which the person who was once a stranger has "now been received into the one holy catholic and apostolic church through baptism. God has made them members of the household of God, to share with us in the priesthood of Christ. Let us welcome the newly baptized."[24]

In the gesture of baptism, we see hospitality being practiced. Baptism becomes a template, a model, for how we are to practice the loving gestures of Christ when he taught us to welcome and include the stranger, making the stranger soon a friend and part of the body of Christ. As baptized members of the Church, we welcome the stranger because of the practice of baptism, in which we who were once not part of the body are now made, by God's grace, a part of the body of Christ.

Jean Vanier, the founder of l'Arche, correctly asserts that a community can only stay alive when new people arrive and commit themselves to it. To invite others, whether strangers or visitors, to live with us is a sign that we are not afraid, that we have some trust in each other.[25] None of us lives forever. Thus it is imperative if a community is to grow, that it commits itself today, tomorrow, and every day to live in community, be community, and welcome others into community. "Welcome is vital for a community. It is a question of life and death," writes Vanier.[26] A community that is not alive, that is stagnant or dying, is one in which being hospitable or welcoming is no longer in practice.

Whose Community Is It Anyway?

One of the more interesting experiences of Christian community and welcoming came while I was living, working, and studying the daily life of the Lambeth L'Arche community. While l'Arche communities began with the inspirational work of Jean Vanier and Pere Thomas in the 1960s, upon the invitation of Pere Thomas for the then-young Vanier to come to know some of the men he was working with in an institution in Compiegne, France, it has largely been people with disabilities who have made it truly their home. Here is the intriguing question: who is the host and who is the guest within a l'Arche community? In the Church, it is usually people who are non-disabled who are the host, and people with disabilities who are the guest. But within the l'Arche communities, the role is often reversed.

Consider this discovery when I was living in l'Arche: I asked a group of people who were the members who are disabled, often called the "core" members, where their home was. Many of the people with disabilities came from institutions or from living with their parents prior to coming into l'Arche. All of the members with disabilities named their "homes" the various l'Arche community homes where they lived. I also asked a group of assistants where their homes were, and they all named off the places where they were either born, or the place where they lived the longest period of their lives. None of them mentioned the homes where they lived currently in the l'Arche community as their "home."

What was novel was this: unlike the various churches that I have visited and been part of or led as a pastor, where it was largely people who are non-disabled who are the ones who are "at home" and the host, with people with disabilities being the guests, in most l'Arche community, it is often the opposite: people with disabilities are the ones who are home, and thus the hosts, and it is people who are non-disabled who are the guests.

What made this switch strikingly clear is when I would visit homes in the L'Arche Lambeth community, as well as other l'Arche communities, in which people with disabilities would welcome me with "Welcome to my home," while people who were non-disabled assistants would welcome me to "The Vine," a name of a house in the L'Arche Lambeth community. The one who was home, the true host of the home, was the person with a disability, and not the assistant who was able bodied. Again: what a wonderful change of roles from the largely able-bodied church. Likewise, the practice of hospitality was often initiated by the person with a disability rather than the assistant, making it that much more fun to watch and be part of after years of being in the role of host. Needless to say, it always took me by surprise . . . but a welcome surprise at that.

Making Room

Lonni Collins Pratt writes the following about hospitality:

> Hospitality isn't about anything as simple as the best china, lace napkins, and crystal wineglasses. It might include those, but the real meaning of hospitality has to do with what one friend called "making room inside yourself for another person."[27]

Throughout our lives, there are moments to make room in our busyness, in ourselves, for other people. As Pratt has noted elsewhere, these moments come quickly, so we must take advantage of them when they appear. Each and every one of us needs a moment of kindness, a little attention, a gesture of welcome and comfort in our faith communities.[28] This is an art, a practice that all of us within the body of Christ—regardless of whether a person is disabled or able-bodied—needs to participate in more often. In an often hostile world, there is a crying need for more spontaneous acts of hospitality, especially among those who are true outsiders.

But surprisingly enough, it may also be the case that the true outsiders who experience the art of hospitality—those with disabilities in the case of this book—may practice the art of hospitality, of comfort, of support, better than others. It is because they know full well what it is to be the recipient of grace gently given and received.

In the next chapter we will consider how, once a person is welcomed over the threshold or through the portal of a community of people, the next step is learning to accept one another just as we are, as members of the body of Christ. This involves the simple action of being able to access the gifts, talents, and services within the body of Christ, though this may be more of a challenge than many would think.

Notes

1. Jean Vanier, *Community and Growth* (Mahwah: Paulist Press, 1979), 168.

2. Vanier, 169.

3. In my other books and articles, I got caught up in the philosophical debate and discussion of what is a "practice," using Alasdair MacIntyre's arguments from *After Virtue* as a norm for understanding a practice, in which he would argue that "football" is a practice while a brick layer art is not a practice because it is simply a part of the larger practice of building a house. Pilgrimage is a practice, according to MacIntyre, with many small parts that need to be performed to engage in the practice of pilgrimage.

But practice may also be a habit or customary performance, such as the practices of a religious community, or to perform or do something repeatedly to perfection, such as welcoming or hospitality.

4. From 1987–1988, I conducted a year-long ethnographic study of l'Arche Lambeth in London, England for my doctoral dissertation from the University of North Carolina—Chapel Hill, in which many stories in this book and other books have found their home.

5. Richard Rohr, *Radical Grace* (Cincinnati: St. Anthony Press, 1975), 29.

6. Ibid., 34.

7. Annie Dillard, *Teaching a Stone to Talk* (New York: Harper Perenniel, 1988).

8. Frederick Buechner, *Wishful Thinking* (New York: Harper & Row, 1973), 6.

9. Rohr, *Radical Grace* 28.

10. Anthony Meisel and M.L. del Mastro, *The Rule of St. Benedict* (New York: Image Book, 1975), 89–90.

11. Christine Pohl, *Making Room* (Grand Rapids: Eerdmans, 1999), 17.

12. Ibid., 31.

13. Martin Marty and Micah Marty, as cited in Lonni Collins Pratt and Father Daniel Homan, *Benedict's Way* (Chicago: Loyola Press, 2000), 65.

14. Pohl, *Making Room*, 29.

15. Ibid., 31.

16. Brett Webb-Mitchell, *Unexpected Guests at God's Banquet* (New York: Crossroad, 1994).

17. Pohl, *Making Room* (Grand Rapids: Eerdmans, 1999), 28–29.

18. Ibid., 17.

19. Harriet McBryde Johnson's obituary; see nyt.com, accessed June 7, 2008.

20. Barbara Brown Taylor, *An Altar in the World* (San Francisco: HarperCollins, 2009), 97.

21. Brett Webb-Mitchell, *Christly Gestures* (Grand Rapids: Eerdmans, 2003).

22. Presbyterian Church (USA), *Book of Common Worship* (Louisville: Westminster/John Knox Press, 1993), 426.

23. Ibid., 413.

24. Ibid., 414.

25. Vanier, 165.

26. Ibid., 169.

27. Lonni Collins Pratt and Dan Homan, *Benedict's Way* (Chicago: Loyola Press, 2000), 69.

28. Ibid.

CHAPTER SIX

Accessibility and Acceptance

*In a Christian community, everything depends
upon whether each individual is an indispensable
link in a chain.* —DIETRICH BONHOEFFER[1]

I love you because God loves everybody!
—BARBARA BROWN TAYLOR[2]

All of us want to be accepted and known.
—LONNI PRATT COLLINS[3]

Stories of Access and Denial

Welcoming others and being hospitable—whether one is part of a religious community that is primarily able-bodied or disabled—seems to be but the first step toward inclusion and genuine integration. Esther de Waal writes:

> . . . hospitality brings us back to the theme of acceptance, accepting ourselves and accepting others, in a most immediate and practical situation which we cannot evade. There is a knock at the door and I have to respond . . . I cannot become a good host until I am at home in my own house, so rooted in my centre (as stability has taught) that I no longer need to impose my terms on others but can instead afford to offer them a welcome that gives them the chance to be completely themselves. Here again is the paradox, that by emptying myself I am not only able to give but also to receive. Filled with prejudice, worry, jealousy, I have no inner space to listen, to discover the gift of the other person, to take down my defenses and be open to what they have to offer.[4]

For the last few decades, churches have struggled with the issue of how to be open and accessible physically to people with disabilities. Accessibility has meant, by and large, having a building and programs that people with disabilities of all kinds can choose to freely to enter.[5] For example, in 1977, the then-United Presbyterian Church (USA) issued a policy paper advocating accessibility to the Church for *all*. The title of this paper was: "That All May Enter." Churches from other Protestant denominations, as well as the Roman Catholic Church, produced similar documents that called for making their churches physically accessible to people with disabilities. Later, many of these same churches went beyond calling for mere physical accessibility by urging that people with disabilities be included both on local church committees and on denominational governing boards, such as the Session of a Presbyterian Church (USA) or a Pastor Parish Committee in the United Methodist Church.

Accessibility shows a level of acceptance by members of a religious community. Accessibility and acceptance seem to go hand in hand: a congregation or parish shows whether or not there is a modicum of welcome and acceptance—in their hearts, minds, and bodies—of people who are disabled, and vice versa by the way a church building, especially a sanctuary is constructed. There seems to be a basic level acceptance of people with disabilities whenever a church building or structure is even partially accessible to people with disabilities. I make this argument because faith communities cannot be forced to build structures that are accessible to people with disabilities. The Americans with Disabilities Act does not apply to religious institutions because of the separation of "church and state," except in the area of employment when it involves separately financed child care services that may receive federal or state dollars. A congregation or parish that is physically and attitudinally accessible is one in which a person(s) with a disability is accepted as a part of a congregation, even to the extent that it influences the design of a building that houses the people of God.

Yet to this day, as I write this book, I know of many churches that are situated around my adopted home towns of Chapel Hill and Carrboro, North Carolina—a liberal bastion of the South that includes some very progressive people with disabilities who raise their concerns without any fear of recrimination—that physically or architecturally block people with disabilities from participating as independently and fully as the able-bodied members of the congregation.

I know this anecdotally. One of my favorite activities when I visit new church buildings or other buildings that house faith communities is to see how many of the "handicapped" parking places are filled with cars. After all, one of the easiest ways to show that a church or other faith community is accessible is by designating those parking spaces closest to a building as "for handicapped people only." Most of these parking spots remain vacant.

At various churches where I was serving as interim pastor, it was sad to see the distance one still had to travel from the designated handicapped parking space to the sanctuary, the educational wing of a church, or the fellowship hall. At one church, a person with a disability would have to get out of their car on a busy street (no parking lot nearby for this church), and if they were in a wheelchair or walker, they would have to traverse the small and steep curb cutaway. Then they had a choice: either take a long series of ramps up to the fellowship hall, or follow the labyrinth-like path of sidewalks across the front yard of the church to an outside elevator, which was equipped with a door that required a key because of the fear of vandalism or abuse by children. This fear was not unfounded. In the short time the elevator had been operational, children had burned out the electrical system once or twice by riding up and down the elevator for their amusement. As a consequence, while the elevator was open every Sunday morning and for special occasions, at any other time a key was needed to operate the elevator.

Once inside the building, the choice for seating for a person with a disability that required a wheelchair or walker was limited to the very front row, a place that most Protestants tend to avoid. There were no pews that were cut shorter so that a person with a wheelchair or walker could choose where he or she wanted to sit. This is why pews are not a friend to many people with disabilities. Movable chairs that can be placed in a way that is comfortable to a person with a disability are preferable to immovable, screwed-into-the-floor pews. Indeed, the history of the pew is that they are a largely Protestant phenomenon. Many medieval cathedrals and basilicas in Europe and the United Kingdom do not have pews, except for those carved into the walls, and their use was restricted to the wealthy or noble class. The general masses of parishioners had either to stand, sit, or lie on the floor wherever they could find a spot.

Physical access into a building is one large hurdle, figuratively speaking, for people in wheelchairs and walkers.[6] For people with visual disabilities, as well as those who may have a motor disability, another issue is access to reading the words of a hymnal, a church bulletin, newsletter, or any other literature. While many congregations in beautiful, historic sanctuaries are reluctant to ruin the architectural lines of their churches, churches that are more non-denominational and newly built are often equipped with large screen projectors and screens. These are a boon to people with visual disabilities and people without the use of arms and hands because the words of the hymns, prayers, or other written documents can be projected onto a screen in enlarged print. As a consequence, those with disabilities can participate along with the rest of a congregation by reading the words projected on the screen.

Access to bathrooms is a whole other discussion. There are many churches that have bathrooms that simply have a big bar attached to one side of the toilet area wall, not necessarily on both sides. Jockeying a wheelchair in the typically small space between toilet doors and wash basins is another problem. As for the doors into these facilities, they are usually not automatic. Ramps are always an intriguing issue. First, as many people in historic buildings will let others know, historic preservation commissions require a review and approval of plans for all ramps, especially when the ramps are visible from the street. That is why many of the ramps into historic church buildings are on the side or back of the church building and are not easily seen. Then there are the issues associated with getting up a ramp and the way a door swings or opens, and whether the door can be operated electronically. I have seen many doors that open outward, toward the person entering in the wheelchair, making it impossible for the person to get into the building. This problem is made more precarious whenever the ramp has a steep pitch, and the person in a wheelchair is feeling the tug of gravity pulling them away from the door. Electric doors that slide open are a welcome sight for some people at the top of the ramp.[7]

While there are examples that show that congregations are willing to invest their hearts, minds, and bodies to make changes to accommodate those with disabilities, what is intriguing is that many of these designs and changes are done without consulting a person with a disability. Not all architects consider asking a person with a disability for design input. For example, at a church's reopening after extensive repairs to the sanctuary that included marble stairs going up to the place where the table and pulpit were located, the designers forgot the need for a ramp for people in a wheelchair. Instead, a crudely built, wooden ramp was added later after the issue was raised by the congregants who used wheelchairs and walkers.

There is another book that can and probably should be written about providing access to communications within a congregation. Options would include providing bulletins or newsletters in Braille or in large print if people wanted a paper draft. For others, there is the option of maintaining an audio connection with those who cannot see during worship but can hear in worship, in which directions of what is happening in worship would be communicated. There is also the option of making it possible for computerized newsletters to be linked to an audio system that makes printed language on computer audible. Increasing the use of hand gestures and sign language for those who cannot hear during worship times, fellowship opportunities, or educational activities; creating a library of resources such as a file of worship services and sermons on podcasts; audio books in church libraries, or utilizing software that can read aloud the news of a church bulletin that is posted on the web; and the utilization of Twitter or Facebook. One final comment: many times a church that makes the structural changes necessary to accommodate people with disabilities is aghast when no one with a disability shows up and uses the facilities. Faith communities often forget the next vital step: welcoming people with disabilities, or advertising that they have made these changes.

Lesson? While the church proudly displays a decal saying it is accessible, in truth, it is anything but accepting or accessible.

Demanding Accessibility: The Example of Harriet McBryde Johnson

Collectively, the foregoing anecdotes provide a sketch of how churches either have or have not been made accessible to people with disabilities. My argument, again, is that accessibility and acceptance are intertwined: places and people that have welcomed and accepted people with disabilities in some form or fashion are congregations that make their building and programs more accessible to people with disabilities.

Part of what has driven this phenomenon of more congregations and parishes welcoming and accepting people with disabilities is the self-determinacy and self-advocacy movement within the disability community. National disability-rights organization like "People First" and "Not Dead Yet" have had a tremendous impact upon society, including the faith communities. While there was a time that many people with disabilities—of all kinds of disabling conditions—were more or less shunted to the side of society, the disability rights movement has brought issues associated with the rights of people with disabilities to the forefront.

One of the leaders of the disability rights movement was Harriet McBryde Johnson. I first met Harriet when I was presenting a paper at a conference at the University of Alabama, discussing the impact of the Americans with Disabilities Act of 1990 on the life of faith communities. After my presentation, a woman in a wheelchair, sitting in the first row, asked me the question: "Do people with disabilities in your denomination have the means to email and blog each other, creating their own network of alliances and friends?" I laughed softly and said, "No. There is no network of people with disabilities who operate freely within the denomination of which I am part." In response, she curtly replied, "Then I have no need of you or your church." And with that, she simply turned her attention away from what I was saying and mentioned nothing else during the rest of my presentation.

The woman in the wheelchair? Harriet McBryde Johnson.

Harriet McBryde Johnson lived with a degenerative neuromuscular disease, the details of which she never wanted to know. She was a lawyer who lived in Charleston, South Carolina, who was known for her engaging conversation with the ethicist and Princeton professor Peter Singer, who argued that fetuses with "drastic disabilities, like the absence of higher brain function or an incompletely formed spine," should be euthanized. Singer argued that infants, like other animals, are "neither rational nor self-conscious . . . Since their species is not relevant to their moral status the principles that govern the wrongness of killing non-human animals that are sentient but not rational or self-conscious must apply here, too."

In rebuttal, Johnson argued that Singer's advocacy of euthanasia boiled down to this: a disability makes a person "worse off. Are we 'worse off"? I don't think so." Then she added: "We take constraints that no one would choose and build rich and satisfying lives within them. We enjoy pleasures other people enjoy, and pleasures peculiarly our own . . . the presence or absence of a disability doesn't predict quality of life."[8]

In November 2003, she wrote of the "Disability Gulag," describing the worse part of institutional life where "wheelchair people are lined up, obviously stuck where they're placed while a TV blares, watched by no one." Johnson called for a de-institutionalization of all people with disabilities into publicly financed home-care settings provided by family, friends, or neighbors.[9] I will be hopeful and add: faith communities too.

How did Johnson see herself? In her obituary, printed in the *New York Times*, it says that she loved to zoom around the streets of Charleston, referring to herself as a "bedpan crip" and "a jumble of bones in a floppy bag of skin." But for many others, she was an inspiration as a person who accepted who she was and what she could and could not do. She took her situation and, to paraphrase her words, she constructed a rich and satisfying life.

Accepting Others and Ourselves

I've been privileged to have known people with disabilities who are pioneers in living a most satisfied life, from Ellen Perry of my community of Carrboro, North Carolina, to the satirist and cartoonist John Callahan of Portland, Oregon, two people who spend a great deal of time in their electric wheelchairs, and from which they speak and write their view of the world. They are people who accept their disability, their limitation, and have constructed an amazing life.

It is one thing to know what it means to be a stranger. It is a wholly other thing to figure out that we are all human, creatures who have amazing gifts and some rather important limitations. While body, mind, and spirit for many of us will continue to function and work with little problem for a great deal of our lives, if we live old enough, we will all face some physical, emotional, relational, intellectual, and spiritual setbacks if not brokenness. Some of us like to think of ourselves as superior. Father Daniel Homan writes that "Jesus says to love others as you love yourself. That's easy. We don't blink at it anymore. But, when we're told to consider others superior, it exposes us. The state of our lukewarm love and our overinflated egos becomes piercingly clear. Jesus says that whoever wants to be first has to be last (see Mark 9:35), that we shouldn't try to get the best seat, and that we shouldn't try to impress others or be impressed too easily (see Luke 14:7–11)."[10] In other words, being humble, or at least having a good assessment of what we can and cannot do, is important in this life.

Richard Rohr writes beautifully not only about being humbled, but of living with all the pieces of life when there is nothing around but our brokenness and the brokenness of other people's lives. We are scandalized by our own brokenness and that of others because we have separated ourselves from the broken character of almost all of reality. Rohr writes:

> When a person who is severely disabled confronts us, we're scandalized and afraid. Everything in our being says, "Oh, it shouldn't be that way, let's change it." But we can't change it. The only thing we know how to do is to draw apart, to pull away in fear, anger, and disappointment with God. But God gives us each other. Those people who are disabled can remind the rest of us who we are. We live under an illusion, thinking we are non-disabled, thinking we've got it together.
>
> We're afraid of those who seem weak because they come with the faces of the crucified Jesus. We push them to the edge of society . . . we shun (people with disabilities) who remind us that our bodies are also one step away, any moment, from crippledness. People with mental disabilities painfully remind us we really aren't very smart.
>
> There is a reason we push all these people far away and far apart. They represent everything we fear and everything we deny about ourselves. Yet to be touched by these people is to discover the deepest recess of our own life.[11]

In her article about the conversation she had with Peter Singer, Harriet McBryde Johnson picks up on Rohr's observation with this powerful statement from the perspective of someone living with a disability:

> He insists he doesn't want to kill me. He simply thinks it would have been better, all things considered, to have given my parents the option of killing the baby I once was, and to let other parents kill similar babies as they come along and thereby avoid the suffering that comes with lives like mine and satisfy the reasonable preferences of parents for a different kind of child. It has nothing to do with me. I should not feel threatened.

Whenever I try to wrap my head around his tight string of syllo-
gisms, my brain gets so fried it's . . . almost fun. Mercy! It's like "Alice
in Wonderland."[12]

What is breathtaking about Johnson's conversation with Singer is
her description of what it felt like deep within her to hear the words of
Singer used in describing her life as a fetus.

Or consider this self-description of her life:

Two or three times in my life . . . I have been looked at as a rare kind
of beauty. There is also the bizarre fact that where I live, Charleston,
S.C., some people call me Good Luck Lady: they consider it propitious to cross my path when a hurricane is coming and to kiss my head
just before voting day. But most often the reactions are decidedly neg-
ative. Strangers on the street are moved to comment:
    I admire you for being out; most people would give up.
    God bless you! I'll pray for you.
    If I had to live like you, I think I'd kill myself.[13]

It is this last comment that is most telling. Most "outsiders" to Johnson's life, like most people I know who first meet a person with a disability, cannot fathom how the person with a disability lives with him
or herself. Despite trying to imagine what it must be like to be disabled,
or what is usually known as the "walk a mile in my moccasins" phenomenon, a person who is non-disabled can probably never understand
what it is like to live with a disability. I confess that I am guilty of leading people in "simulations" of what it might be like to have a disability.
I have placed brown grocery bags over people's heads to simulate constricted vision, cotton balls in their ears to simulate a hearing disability,
and supplied crutches and wheelchairs to simulate immobility. At the
end of the exercise, the person who is non-disabled can remove the bag
or cotton balls, or they can walk away from the chairs and crutches. The
person with a disability cannot.

Like Harriet, and as was true with Rich at the beginning of this book
when he talked openly about living with multiple sclerosis, there is an
authenticity to the narratives of the people who are living with some
kind of diagnosed disability that I've talked to and with throughout the
years. The person with a disability has learned to live with, work around,
accommodate, adapt, and constructed a life well worth living, despite
what some would judge to be a life of "damaged goods," as one ethicist

argued. Accepting the situation at hand, people with disabilities speak with a certain rawness or genuineness, in which the feelings and thoughts of a person are not wrapped in a nice package or sugarcoated. It is raw. It is real. It is vulnerable. It is a place where intimacy of relationships may now enter. And this is something not learned from text books, but by being in situations in which we are given the opportunity to share what it means to live on the margins of life.

In some of my earlier books on issues facing people with disabilities and religious communities, I wrote to a target audience of people with disabilities, to those who were considered outsiders in the community of faith. I write *this* book as an outsider myself. And like others of us who are considered outsiders and are marginalized, many of whom live with disabilities, we carry upon our shoulders a big chip that we more or less dare others to hit, thus letting us vent and fume. Reading parts of Johnson's narrative, as well as meeting her in person, there was a sense of that chip waiting to be hit. This is because many of us who are marginalized live with a certain sense of toxicity or poison in the air we breathe, water we drink, and relationships we keep with our world, our society, our families, and ourselves. Those of us who are marginalized and treated as second class citizens are also tired of fighting and struggling against the dominant or so-called normative culture. We are the ones who do not enjoy the privileges of what society affords others, and thus we are angry and easily depressed because all of who a person or a people might be is not accepted as normal. This is similar to people with any kind of disability: we live in a world that truly does not understand let alone begin to address the sense of frustration and powerlessness that we feel and experience daily.

Jean Vanier has some insights into this phenomenon. He writes that people who are marginalized often live in darkness and often compensate for their anguish with forms of anger. He rightly understands that our anger is a result of the injustices and violence of our past and present, and in some cases foreseeable future. We have particular needs and wants that are not always granted, let alone understood.[14]

Thus what is needed from the community that welcomes and accepts those of us who are marginalized is the following:

First, there must be someone or a community that can listen or receive our story. Second, there must be someone or a community that can be a stable reference, who can encourage, guide, and support a person—with little to no judgment—and bring to that person a sense of security. The community needs to learn how to accept crises, violence, and depression on behalf of the marginalized person. Lastly, the community that is accessible and accepting will need to be a people who are hopeful, self-accepting, and have an ability to sow peace where others have sown discord. After all, a Christian community is "based fundamentally on relationships that are authentic, loving, and faithful, and on which forgiveness and the signs of that forgiveness may be present," writes Vanier.[15] There will need to be healing, not only in each person's life but in the relationships that brought the person pain. In addition, there needs to be the ongoing task of building the community of Christ, the body of Christ. What many people who are marginalized bring to the Christian community is nothing less than the opportunity of being community with one another, and a stronger and healthier community at that.

Truth and Reconciliation

How does a community become a healthier community of faith that can bring together people with disabilities and people who are primarily non-disabled? One of the most important processes that may work is the use of a kind of truth and reconciliation activity in the context of worship.

Over the years, there has been an increase in expression—through voices, songs, pictures, dance, and art work—from people with disabilities that articulate their resentment toward the Church and its slow or lack of action on behalf of people with disabilities. At the same time, the Church lacks information or knowledge about how to engage the community of people with disabilities and, worse, at times there is an attitude of disdain among many church leaders and laypersons. Yet there have been some who have begun to search for a way toward breaking through the wall of resentment and indifference on both sides and reconciling with one another. Here, I offer the proposal that the members who are non-disabled of the body of Christ, the Church, and the community of people with disabilities purposefully engage one another in the joint practice of confessing our faults and sins in love, seeking communal assurance of forgiveness, and passing the peace in a spirit and act of reconciliation. Why? Because God is needed in all human life, and we are called as Christians to discover in what ways the body of Christ is to be an inclusive body that includes people with all kinds or types of abilities or limitations.

South Africa's Truth and Reconciliation Commission provides one example of how societies and communities of faith have broken through and gone over walls that formerly separated people. The Commission demonstrated successfully that by speaking truth, and living truthfully, reconciliation among a people divided can be achieved. As many will recall, the Commission was created in the 1990's so that the victims and perpetrators of violence during the days of apartheid could both give testimony and request amnesty from further prosecution. The cultural mix of the burgeoning democratic government (Nelson Mandela had recently been elected president) with the confessional tradition of the Reformed Church of South Africa made it possible for the once "warring parties" to come together and make amends over their differences. After years of war, bloodshed, angry words, and ruined lives, there came a moment in which peace and reconciliation had a chance of literally and figuratively saving the day.

In a courtroom-like setting, victims and perpetrators alike, both from the African National Congress (ANC) and governmental officials, were given an opportunity to face one another and seek amnesty for past abuses. Some claimed that simply acknowledging the painful tear in the fabric of that society augured peace and reconciliation between the races, ethnicities, and nationalities of that diverse country. What was novel was, first, the commission was granted the power to grant amnesty if the crime had been perpetrated during the apartheid era. Second, neither side was exempt from appearing before the Commission: both the state and the members of the African National Congress were held accountable for past deeds of violence.[16] This model, which was largely confessional, was so successful that it has been adopted by other communities where race has been a stumbling block between people. The example set by the Commission was most recently adopted in Greensboro, North Carolina, when a group of lower-class workers were fired upon by Klansmen and neo-Nazis while they were demonstrating for racial and economic justice on November 3, 1979.[17]

In an ecclesial context, another example of how confessing the truth in love may lead to reconciliation was demonstrated in the former United Presbyterian Church (USA). In the Church's "Confession of

1967," the denomination—as a result of study and a formally approved and adopted theological confessional—acknowledged how racism had been such an integral part of its heritage as people of the Reformed tradition. The Reformed model may provide a way or practice that will enable individual churches to be more inclusive congregations, breaking through the wall that divides the people of God, able-bodied and disabled alike. Through the act of confession, both people with disabilities *and* those who are able-bodied will be given the opportunity to speak or express thoughts and feelings about the insidious nature of the "handicappism" or "ableism" that is alive in congregations and parishes today.

A Theology of Confession

The metaphorical image and idea of breaking through and dismantling walls that separate us is based upon Ephesians 2:14–16, in which the writer, supposedly Paul, addresses the hostility that is found among the people within Ephesus. Paul writes that Jesus "is our peace; in his flesh he has made both groups into one and has broken down the dividing wall, that is, the hostility between us. He has abolished the law with its commandments and ordinances, that he might create in himself one new humanity in place of the two, thus making peace, and might reconcile both groups to God in one body through the cross, thus putting to death that hostility through it." This passage reflects Paul's declaration that the wall between Jews and Gentiles—those who thought they were God's holy consecrated people versus the Gentiles who were seen as being defiled with idol worship—was destroyed, and the people gathered together, through the sacrificial presence of Jesus. The cross addresses and eclipses the "old life," or the old habits and ways, so that a new life, a new humanity, may be born through the instrument of God's love in reconciling us to one another.

As mentioned earlier, the former United Presbyterian Church (USA) in the 1960s created and affirmed "The Confession of 1967" in which it confessed sins of bias and dissension among people based on race. Analogously, much that divided people according to race continues to divide people according to abilities and limitations. As written in the "Confession of 1967," there are times that the church, "guided by the Spirit, humbled by its own complicity and instructed by all attainable knowledge, seeks to discern the will of God and learn how to obey in these concrete situations."[18] Following this affirmation, the "Confession" also states that "God has created the peoples of the earth to be one universal family. In his reconciling love he overcomes the barriers between brothers (sic) and breaks down every form of discrimination based on racial or ethnic difference, real or imaginary."[19]

Let me say as clearly as possible that the same forces that created a barrier between races have created a barrier between people who are considered by the world to be disabled and those who are considered not-disabled. Jesus is "our peace," who has "broken down the dividing wall, that is, the hostility between us" (Eph. 2:14). In God's light, we the members of the body of the risen Christ, are called to receive and uphold one another, including persons with disabilities and people without disabilities.

The "Confession of 1967" continues, stating that because "Jesus identified himself with the needy and exploited, the cause of the world's poor is the cause of his disciples."[20] For the body of Christ to remain indifferent to those who are needy, in this case those with disabilities who have been marginalized and disenfranchised from various parts of Christian community, is to make a "mockery of reconciliation and offers no acceptable worship of God."[21] As we say in the Presbyterian Church (USA), the chief end or purpose of our being created is to glorify God, which is why we need to be about the work of justice by committing ourselves to work for the full inclusion of people with disabilities in every part of the Church.

Liturgy of Confession and Reconciliation

One way that the community of the Church and the community of people with disabilities may begin the process of reconciliation is to have a special worship service in which "Confession" is central to the time of worshipping together. I will demonstrate that we have, in our midst, liturgical resources for moving forward as a church *and* community of people with disabilities *through* confession *toward* reconciliation.

According to "The Service for the Lord's Day," in the Presbyterian Church's (USA) *Book of Common Worship*, the time of Confession follows the Call to Worship, the Opening Prayer, and the Opening Hymn.

In other words, it is one of the first ecclesial acts of a congregation in worship. The theological explanation is that in order to hear the word of God communicated and received aright, we need to be cleansed of our sins—personal and communal—as is explained in the *Book of Common Worship*: "In words of scripture the people are called to confess the reality of sin in personal and common life. Claiming the promises of God sealed in our baptism, we humbly confess our sin."[22] This is reiterated in the Presbyterian Church (USA) "Directory for Worship," in which it is stated that a "Prayer of confession of the reality of sin in personal and common life" are part and parcel of confession.[23]

While this act of confession is part and parcel of a congregation's worship of God, what is being proposed is an entire worship experience that is centered on "Confession and Reconciliation." Following the model of worship of the Presbyterian Church (USA), but easily applied to forms of worship in other denominations, below I outline a possible format for worship:

Call to Worship: A Call to Worship may be written that engages the text from Galatians 3:28, in which there is the acknowledgement that in Christ, there is neither "Jew or Greek, there is no longer slave or free, there is no longer male and female;" nor is there either able-bodied or disabled, for all of us are one in Christ. Indeed, 1 Corinthians 12:12–13 may also be adapted for the "Call" or for "Opening Sentence of Scripture."

Opening Hymn: A good choice may be "In the Midst of New Dimensions," with words and music by Julian B. Rush, whose theme is the reconciliation of opposing sides across many issues.[24]

Confession: In the tradition of the Presbyterian Church (USA), as noted above, this is the time in our worship in which people are to share, communally and personally, the fierce reality of sin in our life. Sin knows no boundary, no category, no classification, and no label: all of us have sinned and fallen short of the glory of God, people who are able-bodied and disabled alike. This may well be an occasion when people with disabilities could list the places, times, and people who caused them great destruction and hurt in a church because they were not welcomed. This act of confession would most likely include the members of the body who are "ableists," participating in the practice of ableism by denigrating, devaluing, and oppressing a person who is disabled. Sometimes the person who is the ableist is non-disabled, but even some people who are disabled can participate in keeping themselves or other people who are disabled opressed because the attitude of "handicappism" is rife in the life of both groups whether it is overt or covert.

It is in this section that it needs to be noted that people with disabilities of any kind are, first and foremost, people. People are people regardless of whether the world deigns them as "non-disabled" or "able-bodied." As I have previously written in this book and books like *Christly Gestures*, there is nowhere in Paul's description of the body of Christ in 1 Corinthians or Romans that people with "disabilities" are not able or capable of performing any role, function, talent, gift or service in the resurrected body.[25]

Assurance of Pardon, followed by the Passing of the Peace, and the Gloria Patri: What is important is not only confession, but the affirmation or assurance that our sins have all been forgiven. A new life has begun in Christ, and it is with this knowledge—which is more than merely intellectual knowing, but a knowing of the heart and body as well—that we are forgiven people, regardless of our abilities or limitations. It is, after all, Christ who makes us this amazingly inclusive body.

Following the words, "Since we have been forgiven in Christ, let us forgive one another," forgiveness is confirmed in the physical touch of hands, arms, legs, and embraces of life with life as we pass the peace of the Christ. In the liturgy, we are all given a chance to be at peace and witness the miracle of the passing of the peace of Christ in our midst.

The beauty of this moment is often skipped by: the peace that is being rendered is not human peace, but Godly peace, the peace of "shalom," which is a gift of God's through Christ. We are to remember that the promise being made here is God's redemption, "and the claims God has on all human life."[26] The assurance of God's forgiving grace is declared in the name of Jesus Christ. We accept God's forgiveness, confident that in dying to sin, God raises us to new life. Furthermore, by practicing the "signs of reconciliation and the peace of Christ . . . we share in the peace, expressing the reconciliation, unity, and love that come only from God, and we open ourselves to the power of God's love to heal our brokenness and make us agents of that love in the world."[27]

This three part movement—confession, assurance, and passing of the peace—becomes the model for how we are to break down the wall that divides people with disabilities from those who are able-bodied in a congregation or parish. This three-part movement involves not only prayer, set within the context of Scripture (opening call), but the very gesture of passing the peace of the living Christ, who sides with those who sense they are oppressed and forsaken.

Later in worship, there is an opportunity to reinforce this movement of confession and reconciliation. For example, in the Scriptures being read, the Old Testament reading may be from Isaiah 43:1–13, which emphasizes what God is calling us to do, bringing forth "the people who are blind, yet have eyes, who are deaf, yet have ears!" (Is. 43:8). In the New Testament reading, along with Epistle readings from either 1 Corinthians or Galatians (already listed in this book), a good choice would be a reading of the parable of the Great Banquet Feast (Luke 14:15–24), or one of the healing narratives.

Preaching or enacting a sermon based upon one of these readings would add profundity to the moment. It is at this time that people with disabilities and those who are able-bodied can "tell their stories," either through verbal means or other artistic expression, such as liturgical dance, visual art, or computer generated message. A time of silent prayer may also be important as people take time to be centered upon the God who is doing a "new thing" in creating a "new heaven and a new earth."

Go Forth into the World

A charge:

In the *Book of Common Worship* there is this instruction or "charge," which is meant to renew "God's call to us to engage in obedient and grateful ministry as God's agents to heal life's brokenness. By the power of the Spirit, we are to be in life and ministry what Christ has redeemed us to be."[28]

The church is called to go forth, "confident that God's rule has been established."[29] God's rule, as expressed in the Scriptures, is that the body of Christ be an inclusive body, for such is the nature of the resurrected Christ. By continually practicing the three acts of confession, assurance, and passing the peace of Christ, we all—regardless of our labels—are given an opportunity to be and become a body that reflects "God's rule" and God's reign, which is for us to live in community with one another, open to the gifts of the body that are embedded in each and every one of us. It is through the acts of confession and reconciliation, lifted up in the sacraments of baptism and Eucharist, that we find ourselves on the pilgrimage of being and becoming the inclusive body of Christ.

Notes

1. Dietrich Bonhoeffer, *Living Together* (New York: Harper & Row, 1954).

2. Barbara Brown Taylor, *An Altar in the World* (San Francisco: HarperCollins, 2009), 103.

3. Lonni Collins Pratt and Fr. Daniel Homan, *Benedict's Way* (Chicago: Loyola Press, 2000), 135.

4. Esther de Waal, *Seeking God: The Way of St. Benedict* (Collegeville: Liturgical Press, 1984), 120–21.

5. This is a contentious issue within and among religious communities. For example, I remember a pioneer in special education arguing in an article and in a paper presentation that buildings should forego ramps and electric doors, and instead place people in strategic spots so that people with disabilities would simply come to a spot, and people would either carry them in a wheelchair to the desired location, or be on the ready to open and shut doors. Indeed, this same pioneer argued that the opportunity of being "community" with one another was being denied by the use of electronic gadgets that allowed people with disabilities to operate independently.

6. Some would argue that this situation of a sanctuary that is largely built for people who are non-disabled is an example of "ableism," which is discrimination against people with disability by people who are non-disabled. The non-disabled sanctuary reflects the "norm" that excludes those people with various disabilities.

7. Interestingly enough, I once heard Dr. Wolf Wolfensberg suggest that ramps were the enemy of community building because when a person in a wheelchair can self-ambulate, he or she does not need a community to be there for and with them. He did not advocate for ramps per se, suggesting that people with disabilities wait upon the community to come and help people in wheelchairs navigate a church's property.

8. See Harriet McBryde Johnson's obituary, nyt.com, accessed June 7, 2008.

9. Ibid.

10. Pratt and Homan, *Benedict's Way* (Chicago: Loyola Press, 2000), 74.

11. Richard Rohr, *Radical Grace* (Cincinnati: St. Anthony Messenger Press, 1995), 85–86.

12. Harriet McBryde Johnson, "Unspeakable Conversations," *New York Times Magazine*, February 16, 2003.

13. Ibid., 2.

14. Jean Vanier, *Community and Growth* (Mahwah, NJ: Paulist Press, 1979), 170–72.

15. Vanier, 174. For Vanier's Catholicism, the exemplar of such healing is the priest, but for Protestants it is in the life of the community itself.

16. "Truth and Reconciliation Commission in South Africa," Wikipedia, accessed on http://en.wikipedia.org/wiki/Truth_and_Reconciliation_Commission _%28South_Africa%29, accessed March 12, 2010.

17. On-line reference, "Greensboro Truth and Reconciliation Commission." http://www.greensborotrc.org, accessed March 12, 2010.

18. "The Confession of 1967", *The Book of Confessions* (Louisville, KY: Presbyterian Church (USA), 2004), 9.01–.56.

19. Ibid., 9.44.

20. Ibid., 9.46.

21. Ibid., 9.46.

22. *Book of Common Worship* (Louisville: Westminster/John Knox Press, 1993), 35.

23. *Book of Order* (Louisville: Office of the General Assembly, 2005), W-3.3301.

24. In the book *Sing the Faith* (Louisville: Westminster/John Knox Press, 2003), Hymn no. 2238.

25. Brett Webb-Mitchell, *Christly Gestures* (Grand Rapids: Eerdmans, 2003), Part I.

26. *Book of Common Worship*, 35.

27. Ibid., 35, 36.

28. Ibid., 44.

29. Ibid., 45.

CHAPTER SEVEN

Inclusion and Gesture

I used to try to explain that in fact I enjoy my life,
that it's a great sensual pleasure to zoom by in my power
chair on these delicious muggy streets (of Charleston, SC),
that I have no more reason to kill myself than most people.
But it gets tedious. God didn't put me on this street to
provide disability awareness training to the likes of them.
—HARRIET McBRYDE JOHNSON[1]

Inclusion as Co-Creation

The previous chapter focused on accessibility and acceptance, and this
"move" is necessary for the final push toward inclusion. After all, the very
title of this book, *Beyond Accessibility*, proposes that accessibility *into* the
life of a faith community's buildings, programs, and activities, by and
with people with disabilities, is a part of the process *toward* full inclusion.

An example of full inclusion comes from the world of theater. My
friend Richard Reho is moving with great ease in a room with other
women and men, some of whom are considered able-bodied, while a
few others are considered "disabled," simply asking them to move arms,
fingers, hands, and bodies. Richard is the engine behind the Community
Inclusive Theater Group, which brings together performers who are disabled with those who are non-disabled to co-create over many months
a theatrical piece. Some with effort and others moving almost effort-
lessly, they trade off the role of who will direct or guide the next set of
movements. They move to a pianist's improvisation, the pianist herself
watching the movement of bodies, as they are all in a creative dance
together, being led by the energy that is present in the movement of creative souls.

They are co-creating this play, this creation, of which they are the co-creators.

Co-creation in this theatrical piece is highly unusual, tender, transparent, and genuine. There is not a right or wrong way of doing anything. For those actors who are non-disabled, there are moments of great frustration as they want to be directed by a director, told where to go on stage, told how to read a line, told how to think about a character. But in co-creating this act of theater, inclusive of one and all, there is no preset script, music, or choreography. There is only the script that comes out of conversations with each other and in the act of playing with one another in a large, sparse rehearsal room. There is no music per se, except the music that may be written or composed when all the players are working together on the music of their own hearts, minds, and bodies. And the choreography and stage directions come only from the group moving together in a rehearsal room over a period of time. There is only a sort of unselfconscious interaction occurring between performers, director, and pianist. And in the midst of it all, there is an atmosphere of acceptance, creating space for a rich interplay between performers of differing abilities and limitations.

There are two outstanding moments in a documentary film made of this theatrical group. One is the intricate hand gesture of Laura, a young woman with autistic behaviors, which in the outside world would look strange and ritualistic. In the context of theater and dance, it is a gesture that is expressive and beautiful. Megan Jones, a poet who lives with a learning disability, writes and speaks her mind in the documentary:

> In our little ways
> We are moving the universe
> Because we can.

The second outstanding moment in the documentary is Richard's movement with Chris. Chris is a young man with severe cerebral palsy. He was thought to be developmentally delayed or intellectually challenged because of his inability to speak or use hand signs but actually he is quite bright and creative, though he uses an alternative form of communication. Richard asks Chris if they could work together to choreograph a dance in the play. And with Chris's simple nod of the head "yes," Richard envelops Chris in his arms and draws him close to his body. Then slowly, artfully, tenderly, with Chris simply moving his head to the right and to the left, or up and down, moving an arm a certain direction, or his torso, Chris directs Richard where to move his body, arms, legs, head and torso. In the swirling, centrifugal force of the two moving together in the élan of the dance it is emotionally gratifying to watch the two become one in this co-creation, co-creative dance.

Coming out of a discussion with Richard, watching the movie, and having participated in an open-ended creative period with similar gatherings of people who are non-disabled and people with disabilities, the questioning begins: What would happen if worship were similar to the dance? What or how would "education" be understood and be enacted if we embraced an educational or discipleship process that was led by the Gospel, perhaps according to the lectionary cycles? Could we learn ways we *all* can live and practice the Gospel or the Jesus-like gestures of the Christian tradition, learned and re-learned together with people of all or any kind of disabling condition? After all, the entire theatrical piece was dependent upon gestures of body, mind, and spirit, from the graceful movement of limbs and torsos to the gestures of language in thoughtful speech acts. My mind didn't stop whirling: what about fellowship in which people communicated in ways that others understood, perhaps using sign language, or other means of communication like art, dance, or poetry? How would our understanding of service, of working on behalf of and with others in their own behalf, change or be modified with the inclusion of people with disabilities who are often seen as the objects or target of charity? The act of people with disabilities serving others in service projects could change how many in the body of Christ perceive their "powerlessness." Suddenly, people with disabilities are disabled no more, but are the able-bodied ones. Imagine the possibilities of changing lives in, among, and with others in the body of Christ in which the power of the Holy Spirit is assumed to be distributed generously to one and all, for the greater, common good of the body present in our churches!

Educating for Full Inclusion

Learning to be and become a faith community, or specifically the body of Christ-as-church with each other—regardless of our abilities or limitations—is going to take more than a single Sunday morning ritual of worship that is dedicated to and centered on "disability awareness," though this would be a good beginning for many churches. Indeed, every Sunday is really "dis-ability Sunday" in worship as we all come with our limitations and finite set of abilities. Each of us is un-able or "dis-able" in some fashion within the body of Christ. It is primarily the responsibility of each person, with the assistance of others in a faith community, to discover what or who they are; to develop the gestures that embody their gift, talent, and service; and to use those gestures for the benefit of the community.

Once people with a disability—people with all types of disabilities, of both genders, and of all ages—have been welcomed within the confines of a congregation or parish, they confront a new challenge: the challenge of educating, forming, shaping, or creating a discipline or practice by which the body of Christ may more fully include those who are disabled alongside people who are non-disabled in the ongoing activities and pro-grammatic life of communities of faith. As has already been noted in this book, changing attitudes and going beyond accessibility to reach full and equal participation of *all* members, in all areas of communal life, is the last barrier to be crossed before achieving full inclusion. It is an issue of justice as well as simply educating members of a church to understand the God-given gifts of people with disabilities, along with the necessity of adapting to the presence of people with disabilities who are called by God in Christ to be part of the body of Christ and thus are not leaving the confines of a church.

Herein lies the next step of the Church's pilgrimage toward full inclu-sion: moving beyond simply welcoming people with disabilities into the life of a church, treating people with disabilities under the category or special event of "disability ministry," where people with disabilities are being separated because of their disability into separate worship, separate education programs, separate fellowship opportunities, and being the focus of mission efforts. The goal is to treat people with disabilities not as a "special ministry"—with separate worship, education, and fellowship opportunities—but as full, active, voting members of a faith community. The challenge is the full integration or inclusion of people with disabil-ities in worship, education, fellowship, youth and small group activities, choir or music programs, art programs, service opportunities, and mis-sion programs. Again, moving toward inclusion will involve confronting the awkwardness that some church members experience in learning to be with those who are not like them. Both the person who is non-disabled and the person with disability will need to get beyond feeling uncomfortable and awkward in each other's presence. Overcoming the challenge of full and total inclusion of people with disabilities into the Church is going to take some time.

How do we teach a congregation or parish the first step or stage of moving beyond mainstreaming approaches—in which people with disabilities are provided separate-but-equal worship opportunities, educational programs, and activities that incorporate a mainstreaming approach of people with disabilities—toward full, co-creative, inclusion of people with disabilities as equal partners in God's service in the active life of a church? In the following sections I will, first, consider one of the key obstacles toward full inclusion of people with disabilities in the life of the church: the way we educate *all* members in the body of Christ. Since all education is context dependent—education looks different and is defined differently dependent on the context in which it occurs—the question before us is this: how do we understand the basic nature of being Church and Christ-like with each other *regardless* of labels and categories of abilities or limitations? This has to do with the ecclesiological perspective of what is called "the Church," and whether the Church is a verbal, linguistic, and intellectual phenomenon—an extension of the academy—or also organically and spiritually based as the body of Christ. Recall that we explored the theme of the body of Christ in the first half of this book. So what does life in a church look like when the presumption is that church members are not part of any old body of believers, but part of the mysterious yet real resurrected body of Christ?

What follows is this: how do we educate the *entire* membership of the body of Christ, able-bodied and disabled alike, together, at the same time, in the same place? After all, Paul did not classify people by their abilities or limitations as to which members will be teachers, caregivers, or healers in the body; the Spirit decides. Perhaps in reconsidering, and reclaiming, the ancient but eternal vision of the Church as the body of Christ, we may discover in what ways we are all inextricably part of the body of Christ, able-bodied and disabled alike.

The Church as School

One of the key obstacles toward full inclusion of people with disabilities in the Church is not only the way we perceive and thus construct our worship of God, but the way we understand education in the context of the Church. The Church is the body of Christ and what the Benedictines understand as the "school for God's service."[2] To quote Michael Casey: "[we] as individuals and as members of a group . . . are to learn Christ"[3] in this church-as-school.

When hearing or reading the word "school," many people in the church revert to how they were and are taught in Sunday school, youth groups, and seminaries. We were and are taught to understand education in what John Westerhoff would often call a "schooling-instruction paradigm," where there is a time, place, and practice considered "education" in the otherwise separate and hectic life of a church. In other words, education in a church is often an extension of the way we are educated in other contexts that give themselves the name "school." Christian education is typically held in rooms reserved for this purpose in an educational wing or hallway of a church. Curriculum (paper), activities, and media aids (film projectors, PowerPoint presentations, and tape recorders) are provided and classes are held during an hour that is set apart from the other distinct activities of the church, such as worship, preaching, choir rehearsals, counseling, administration, biblical studies, fellowship, prayer, or service projects. The content of these classes is focused primarily on biblical history, theology, and the philosophy of the church, taught largely through linguistic communication modes.

The usual "fifty-minute hour" of Sunday school instructions is largely based upon what Paul Freire called the "banking concept" of education. Here, the teacher gives information pertinent to the context to students who sit and receive education passively. A teacher's lecture or leadership—chalk and talk, repetitive drills, homework, completion of fill-in-the-blank or solve-the-puzzle worksheets and the rote memorization of biblical verses, creeds, and confessions—constitutes the core activities of the class. In many cases, the student then simply echoes the material on worksheets, and depending on the context, sometimes brings home a small hands-on souvenir or worksheet from the educational activity found in the pages of the Sunday school packet. Freire called this process of education "dehumanizing" since there is no connection between a person's life and the knowledge accumulated. The teacher simply pours the information into the mind of the student, and waits for it to be spit back out. Although reading, listening to lectures, studying, and memorizing Scripture have their worthy places in education in general, such approaches may ultimately fail because they do not create a connection with the rest of one's life. In other words, someone needs to connect the dots for students between what is learned in the culture called "school" and the culture called "life."[4]

The problems with conventional Sunday schools (Protestant) and catechetical instructions (Catholic) are six-fold:[5] First, the school's context—the Bible, church history, and theology—did not and still may not make a connection with our lives in the growing complexity of today's world. This lack of connection is because we have reduced the great ongoing story that we Christians are part of to objective tidbits and consumable "factoids," or "memory verses." Not enough can be written about the need to make the learning process relevant to the lives of Christians in the body of Christ, including both teacher and learner.[6]

Second, by using the educational material in a way that discounts the person's life, we assume that a person is a blank slate to be written on rather than a life already being lived. This can fail to inspire a dialogue between teachers and students, thus "killing off the passion" of students because they become passive learners as they are fed a steady diet of facts.

Third, the current approach to learning in the church is directed toward the individual and not necessarily toward the community as a whole. Christian religious education and worship in particular are beholden to the viewpoint that some people are in search of the community for what it can bring to them, rather than seeking a community in which they give of themselves—where each person's life is open to the other, without hesitation.[7]

Fourth, there is a loss of the communal or corporate memory. Basic knowledge of the Bible, church history, and theology has been lost among generations of Christians. Many people are not loyal to the faith communities in which they were raised. "Reading, writing, and memorization" of biblical verses have become consumable commodities, rather than occasions to engage us.

Fifth: in much of education in the Church, we seem more interested in education-as-entertainment than in education-as-transformation. There is the absence of training the body and the spirit along with the mind and the emotions. Christian education, as constructed today, is meant to be a pleasing, emotionally satisfying experience for both the teacher and the learner, rather than transformational of both the life of the teacher and student. "Rather than being focused on praising God, the Church at worship and in educational programs has been captured by the desire to "entertain" and market a successful "product" that meets the psychological, emotional, and therapeutic needs of the learner.

Sixth and finally, people who are severely or profoundly disabled are grouped into their own, separate classrooms or worship services. This is a recurrent problem that I have encountered in meetings of church groups, at conferences on disability issues, and with the individual parishes that I consult with. In many instances, the parents, family members, and friends of those with developmental disabilities or who are severely or profoundly multiply disabled see the provision of separate classrooms and worship positively. They tell of how their loved one finds companionship in the group and how family and friends get a much needed break or respite during a Sunday morning worship. Many of those with these disabling conditions also find a new community of friends sometimes as well in these separate gatherings. Parents have argued with me that grouping the disabled together is an example of "like attracting like." For the same reason, the members who are non-disabled of congregations do not want to welcome people with disabilities in their midst during worship or Christian education activities and programs, saying "they aren't like us; they won't understand what is going on." The focus has been on what can be known theologically as an intellectual activity, rather than sharing a common vision of education as an activity that involves one's mind, body, and spirit in learning and practicing the fine art of being and becoming a community of Christians with one another.

Separating people with similar disabilities into their own groups is a residue from the days of institutionalization, when the powers-that-be grouped people with similar disabilities in large groupings. However, many studies have shown that while we are all attracted to like-minded people, there is more potential for growth, change, and conversion when we are with people who are not like us. Studies have shown how young people who were thought to be severely or profoundly disabled grew educationally, emotionally, and socially in the company of able-bodied children. I still remember from my undergraduate internship experience in a mainstreamed classroom watching a young child in a wheelchair who, one day after watching her classmates drink from a water fountain, suddenly and without prompting or practice maneuvered a hand that we thought unusable to the bar that caused the water fountain to work, shooting herself with water in the face and finally the mouth. The acquisition of this skill wasn't even on her Individualized Education Plan! Likewise, I have watched children who gathered every Sunday for a children's sermon make way for a child using Canadian crutches, and signing to the same child—who was also hearing impaired—without any instruction from the pastor. The children had learned sign language in public schools, and were using it spontaneously now in the church setting. Partially as a result of such experiences, my bias in this book is for full, inclusive education, which will benefit *all* rather than a select few, in learning to be and become members of the body of Christ.

Most educational approaches in the Church assume that knowledge of God, Christ, the Spirit, and the precepts of the Church, are largely based on intellectual propositions which utilize one's cognitive skill, rather than a practice-based form of knowledge which engages and is based upon the utilization of one's mind, body, and spirit. An intellectual-only approach to educating Christians is especially true among Protestant Christians, whereas more Roman Catholic and Orthodox Christians, represented by the Greek and Russian Orthodox Churches, have focused more on the bodily rituals of the Christian life. The intellectual-only approach to educating Christians will never be inclusive by its very nature because it is based on language and cognitive skills, skills at which some people may not be as proficient. This leads to the following question: What would a more inclusive approach to educating in the body of Christ look like?

A Different Approach to Education: Educating toward Full Inclusion

In order for people with disabilities to be fully included in the Church, the first task at hand is to define what it means to be "Church." As stated earlier, if the church is a place where members spend a great deal of time intellectualizing about propositions concerning the Christian life, then people with disabilities, especially with intellectual or developmental disabilities, will be marginalized and segregated because they are not capable of participating in some intellectual activities. While it may seem like a harsh judgment, there is little chance that people who are able-bodied, and who participate in a highly intellectual understanding of their faith, will often tolerate—let alone move toward—accommodating people who are severely or profoundly developmentally delayed or intellectually challenged. Again, this is why worship, educational programs, special events, service projects, even fellowship time, may find some people with disabilities marginalized and thus secluded from the majority of the members who are able-bodied in a Church.

As an alternative to the dominant, intellectualized approach to Christian education and worship, there is another way of perceiving, and thus living life in and as the body of Christ, in which full inclusion of people with disabilities with those who are non-disabled is possible: embracing and reclaiming our identity as members of the body of Christ. Rather than the schooling-instruction paradigm of education, or the banking-concept of education, the focus is on a socialization or enculturation approach to educating Christians in the traditions, rituals, and practices of the storied life of faith. According to Thomas Groome, "becoming Christian requires the socializing process of a community capable of forming people in Christian self-identity. We 'become Christians together.'"[8]

Why is this approach significant for people with disabilities? While people with disabilities will always be excluded from a community of faith that adheres to the schooling-instructional paradigm for educating believers, the socialization-enculturation approach of educating people into the practices of the body of Christ offers people with disabilities a chance *not* to be excluded from the overall practices of the Church. In this section, there will be, first, an exploration of the church-is-the-body-of-Christ, and the impact this theological truth may have on the overall way we learn and teach in the body of Christ. Second, what do we practice in the body of Christ? We practice the gestures of Christ. Third, in the very performance of gestures we learn the virtues of the Church, which in turn teach us the habitual practices of being God's people, able-bodied and disabled alike.

A Theology for Christian Education

To recap Part I, the body of Christ is not just like any other body, physical or social, regardless of one's philosophical or theological assumptions. *This* body is the body of Jesus Christ, the risen Son of God, in whom we encounter God through fellowship and communion with other Christians. Christ's body is not a human body per se, but is a kind of reflective realism. That is, the Church as Christ's body reflects attributes of the human body in certain ways but not in others, as I will explain momentarily. Janet Skokice argues that theological models such as "body of Christ" must be understood contextually. That is, "body" is a way of talking about Christ's activity. "Body of Christ" appears in Paul's letters more often than any other metaphor for describing what the church is. Not long after Paul wrote his letters, speaking of the Church as Christ's body became a part of the Christian community's common vocabulary, embellished over generations of Christians and giving each generation a context of Christian reflection.[9]

Re-imaging the Church as the body of Christ, no matter how big or small our congregation or parish, means that we are *in* and participants *of* the works of love that are unique to the resurrected body of Christ. Because we are part *of* Christ's body, there are some unique aspects of being members of the body. First, we are made up of the same "stuff" as Christ himself.[10] Writing in a culture that was shaped by the early Greek philosophers, Paul used concepts and language that come from those philosophers. Like the Greeks, who assumed that human bodies were made of the same "stuff" as the world around them—such as air, earth, water, and fire—it is probable that Paul and the early Church believed that its members were a microcosmic synthesis of the larger body of Christ: members' lives are made with and of the same "stuff" as Christ himself. And that "stuff" is none other than the Spirit. Paul understood that Christ's body is porous as the Spirit of God moves freely within this social body. Jesus is to have said that the "wind blows where it chooses, and you hear the sound of it, but you do not know where it comes from or where it goes. So it is with everyone who is born of the Spirit" (John 3:8). The Holy Spirit blows in and around our lives, wherever the Spirit wills.

As we saw earlier in part one, there is an authoritative structure to this body, in which the head—namely, Jesus Christ—is truly the topmost or central part of the body that rules the rest of the body.[11] In Paul's description of the body in his first letter to the Corinthians, he writes that the mind of Christ is central to the body of believers: "For who has known the mind of the Lord so as to instruct him? But we have the mind of Christ" (1 Cor. 2:16). This means that we are all dependent not only upon the other members, but upon the head of the body, Jesus Christ: "We must grow up in every way into him who is the head, into Christ" (Eph. 4:15).[12]

If Christ is the head of the body, we, the members, make up the rest of the body. Paul never tells us that the body of believers replaces Christ's body, nor that it represents Christ's body, nor even that it is Christ's mystical body. God is still here, just as real and physical as God was and is in Jesus Christ. If it is true that we are members of Christ's body, then God's presence in the world today depends very much on us.

For example, what are we to make of Paul's example of the ear saying to the eye, "I do not belong to the body because I am not an eye" (1 Cor. 12:16)? Are we to consider it an account of friction within the Corinthian church, in which Paul used the language of his time and tradition to explain both the reality of living in the body of Christ and in the presence of Christ himself? I propose that this is a way of talking about the experience within the body of Christ that occurs when a group of people, because of their place and function within the body, excluded another group. Paul charges the church to practice respect among the members of Christ's body. This is the way of Christ, which we know through his earthly ministry, in which God was and is among us. Christ is still with us as we mediate him to the world. The power of God flowing through us is how God acts through those who are being changed to live according to Christ's image.[13]

Gifts and services of Christ's body extend to one and all, regardless of ability or limitation.[14] Every member of the body—able-bodied and disabled alike—has been given a gift (*charisma*, meaning grace-given), by the Holy Spirit. And every gift is of equal dignity. As John Howard Yoder writes, "Each bearer of any gift is called, first of all, to reciprocal recognition of all the others, by giving 'special honor to the less comely members.'"[15] This is significant insight because it points to the deeper mystery of Christ's body, where all who are baptized—women and men, poor and rich, disabled and non-disabled, gay and straight, young and old, of all ethnic heritages—are bearers of God-given gifts and services for the good of Christ's body. Therefore, one goal of the body of believers in our congregations should be to aid others in discovering, naming, and growing into their gift. By doing so we become a church that embraces a Pauline vision of "every-member counts empowerment, where there would be no one un-gifted, no one not called, no one not empowered, and no one dominated. Only that would live up to Paul's call to 'lead a life worthy of our calling.'"[16]

It is important here to say that Paul was not using metaphorical or analogical language, writing that the church is *like* a body, or the Church *as* the body of Christ. He was claiming something more forceful: the church *is* the body of Christ (See both 1 Cor. 12, and Romans 12). And in this body, the Spirit of God does not choose to neglect or not be in the life of people whom the world calls disabled, let alone in the distribution of gifts, services, and talents in the body of Christ. None of the gifts of the Spirit are withheld or designated to people based upon one's academic pedigree, I.Q., social adaptation scale, or any other modern assessment tool. Yoder reminds us that we cannot take selfish pride in our accomplishments because all our accomplishments, gifts, and services are God-given.[17]

If the Spirit of God is what unites us as one body in Christ, how do we learn about the practices or the gestures of this body? Wouldn't it be in the context of a community, in which we are all to work together toward the up-building of each other—disabled and able-bodied alike? In other words, education in the body of Christ, given the truth that it is based upon the body itself, is to be inclusive. In this next section, I argue for a more inclusive approach to educating people with disabilities and those who are non-disabled in the body of Christ.

Inclusive Education in the Body of Christ

An educational approach that is based upon the "chalk and talk" method, which groups people according to abilities and the understanding of biblical facts and theological propositions, will continue to segregate those who are able-bodied and people with disabilities. Whenever and wherever education is separated from worship, and service is separated from fellowship, each part of the church becomes its own entity and the body of Christ is fractured.

Here is the shift of understanding education in the context of the Church: if one assumes a congregation or parish in its current situation, where education is cut off from worship, and service is cut off from worship, as is fellowship, and each part of a church is an entity unto itself, then the body is fractured. However, if a church is to embrace the idea that it *is* the body of Christ, and is to become a place where worship-education-fellowship-service are integrated with one another toward learning to live the Jesus-life, a practical question is: What is education in the body of Christ? And how does education take place in the context of the body of Christ? More specifically: How do we educate people with disabilities in the body of Christ?

Again, as we described earlier in this book, consider the following: the surrounding society created special schools for persons with disabilities, and segregated classrooms within public schools for people with disabilities. So too did the Church. We created special classrooms for people with disabilities, and special churches and chapels on the grounds of state institutions. To this day, there are still special worship services for people with developmental disabilities throughout the country, held at different times and places than Sunday morning worship. Likewise, there are still segregated Sunday school classes with special curriculum that mirror the material written and the approach taken during the 1950s and 1960s in American society.

In the 1970s, many school districts approached special education through a "mainstreaming" approach. Mainstreaming involved the following practice: placing a child with a disability into a public classroom with his or her peers throughout most of the day, making no special adaptations per se in the classroom itself, and offering remedial courses in another corner of the classroom or a special education classroom in another part of the building. Again, the Church in many ways followed this approach, merely placing a person with a disability in Sunday worship, Sunday school, adult Bible studies, and youth groups, with no adaptations on behalf of the person with a disability or accommodations by the congregation per se. This approach perpetuated an "us" versus "them" mentality.

From the late 1980s to today, inclusion and inclusivity became the "catch-words" of the education strategy of special educators and social activists in the "disability" community. Instead of placing a child or a young adult in a standard classroom for all or part of the day, and expecting the student to keep up, inclusion involved rearranging not only the classroom's physical layout, but the entire curriculum and class of students as well. The idea behind inclusive education in the Church is this: once a classroom is inclusive, it will have been re-thought and re-structured, serving a cluster of people with disabilities, not just a single person. The goal? To see that people with disabilities and those who are not disabled will not only see and hear but relate to one another not as "us" versus "them", but as "we," for we all benefit from learning, worshiping, and praying together.[18]

Learning With and Through Gesture

In the body of Christ what we are learning together are the gestures of Christ. While much education in the life of the Church has focused on the habits of the heart and mind, an emphasis on the body is also necessary. How do we teach the habits of hospitality, goodness, and love in ways that go beyond teaching the mind and spirit? It is when we focus on the gestures in the body of Christ that we are capable of bringing in people with disability. Education for people with physical, emotional, behavioral, visual, auditory, or developmental disabilities often begins with their bodies: the crafting of intentional movement from an array of possible actions.[19]

What is a gesture? A gesture is a fusion of mind, body, and spirit in Christ's one body by means of a physical act. Gestures are learned, practiced, and performed by members of Christ's body. The community of Christ is recreated by the gestures that embody the story of God's gospel. Some gestures are specific to an individual's grace-given gift and service in Christ's body. Others are performed in common and in coordination with other members of Christ's body. And there are some gestures that are performed within the context of worshipping God. Scripture, the traditions of a church's denomination, and the traditions of a parish or congregation where the gestures are performed, provide a narrative context for the gestures. The authenticity of any gesture requires it to be a performance of Scripture itself, as interpreted within the context of Christ's one body. Because of each gesture's origin, gestures both have a story and embody a story; the gestures share that story with others, passing it down to the next generation of Christians.[20]

Patterning, Performing, and Practicing the Gestures

In Paul's letter to Titus he writes about "patterning" what is good and right in the way of Christ: "Urge the younger men to be self-controlled. Show yourself in all respects a pattern of good works and in your teaching show integrity, gravity, and sound speech that cannot be censured"

(Titus 2:6–8). Likewise, Dietrich Bonhoeffer writes that Christ is to be the "pattern that we must follow as we walk as he walked, do as he has done, and love as he has loved.[21] By patterning, we are to set before us the example of how we are to live as Christians, namely through the detailed actions of Jesus during his ministry upon this earth—as well as the instructions in Paul's Epistles—and use them as a "recipe book" of sorts for how or what we are to perform. Patterning is thus the first stage or step in learning a gesture, setting before us a concrete example of someone who is a master at performing a gesture in the body of Christ.

For example, when teaching or re-teaching someone how to share an object with another person or a group of people, the gesture begins by someone holding an object that one wants or needs. Reading the story of "love your neighbor as yourself" from the Gospels, one is asked to slowly relinquish what is in one's hand to another person, even when the impulse might be to hold it as one's own.[22]

A gesture and the act of patterning gestures is more co-creative when it is determined by a group, rather than being defined by a fixed idea of how Christ might have performed it. When an entire group—of both those with disabilities and those who are able-bodied—participate, gestures that can be used by all can be co-created. The gesture of "sharing" that we visited above exemplifies a process:

- *Inspire Participation of All.* Instead of a teacher or pastor showing a student the gesture of sharing, begin by exploring gestures of what sharing could look like among people in a group. In the co-creative process, this initial move is to inspire participation by all.[23]

- *Select an Appropriate Gesture.* For a group working on "sharing," the group would decide what is the best or most appropriate gesture of sharing that is most applicable to the entire group.

- *Connect with Other Creative Gestures.* Beginning with gestures of sharing, the group could discuss what other virtues or moral ideals could be connected with the gesture of sharing?

- *Share the Results Widely.* Be sure that everyone has a chance to participate in and practice the gesture of sharing, along with other gestures that may lift up a connective web of Christ-*like* gestures that can be shared with others, like a gesture of welcome, of hospitality, or of peace.

• *Continue to explore.* Investigate and create additional gestures outside of the educational or worship moment, bringing them to the group's gathering the next time it meets.

Once a group selects the appropriate gesture from this co-creative process, let others know the example to be imitated, moving from simple to more complex practices, with a tutor or mentor by the side of those learning the gestures. This will take the efforts of a community working in unity with their hands, minds, and spirits as they take apart and re-connect the lessons of being Church with one another. After all, as Ronald Rolheiser reminds us, Christ wants from us not admiration but imitation, not like a mime on a street corner but undergoing "his presence so as to enter into a community of life and celebration with him . . . as Christ is a presence to be seized and acted upon."[24]

Eventually, we move from awkward first performance and practice to habitual, ritualistic movements. In imitating Christ, we find ourselves moving from once-awkward gestures to now "holy habits." Thomas Aquinas says that habits are acquired dispositions that form us "all the way down, at the level of the body, the will, and the intellect, shaping our entire being."[25] By practicing and performing the gestures of Christ often enough, they become habit, making it possible for us to produce an infinite number of gesture-bound practices that are diverse and able to be used in a myriad of situations and places.

Being and Becoming the Gesture

In the end, our habit or way of being in the world, shaped by our Christian gestures, makes us gesturers of the Word of God, and the living Word that is Christ. Jesus performed many gestures in God's name: he healed the sick, cared for the poor, proclaimed the goodness of God's realm, and enacted the Word in his charitable, grace-filled gestures. As gesturers and co-creators we all—whether people who are able-bodied or disabled—can participate and perform the gestures we were called to enact as part of the body of Christ. Performing the gestures of the body of Christ, we embody Christ for others in this world. Christ has no hands but our hands in reaching out to those who need assistance, just as we need his hands when we ourselves feel fragile, or his arms when we feel alone.[26]

The educational goal of the Gospel is simple: we are to have the stamina of character to perform the gestures of Christ, seeing this world as God's creation, and listening to the Gospel as if Christ were present among us today. Educating disciples and practicing a certain discipline based upon the gestures of Christ through a co-creative process may not be easy, clean, or orderly at times. But in the chaos, God is present in the simplest of gestures that we all can perform—people who are able-bodied and disabled alike—in acts of love in the all-inclusive body of Christ.[27]

Notes

1. Harriet McBryde Johnson, "Unspeakable Conversations," *The New York Times Magazine*, February 16, 2003, 2.

2. A more complete critique is found in Brett Webb-Mitchell, *Christly Gestures* (Grand Rapids: Eerdmans, 2003), Introduction.

3. This entire critique comes from my book *Christly Gestures* (Grand Rapids: Eerdmans, 2003), Part I.

4. Webb-Mitchell, *Christly Gestures*, Part I.

5. Ibid.

6. The above critique of church-based Christian education is broad, and includes educational programs for people who are non-disabled and disabled alike. However, there is one other problem for people with intellectual or developmental disabilities and Christian religious education. Relying on paper curriculum, and, in many cases, simple memorization training of Bible verses in much of the literature, the current literature tends to do the following: to begin, the class of people with disabilities is set aside as a separate educational context, apart from others who might be of the same age-range, but not intellectual abilities. In other words, there is a segregated educational approach in terms of people with disabilities in educational church-based programs. Next: the material for people with intellectual disabilities is simply first or second-grade based educational material, in which often times only the images on the curriculum have changed to what is given to those who are chronologically younger. Finally: much of the material is either based upon memorization or simple hands-on, experiential activities, which fail to be part of a larger educational opportunity with people of the same age as the person with a disability. In some cases, some church-based Sunday schools are now more "mainstreamed," meaning that the participant with a disability is included in age-appropriate classes for some activities, but moved over to a corner of the same room with a "best buddy" tutor who is a person who is non-disabled for the majority of the Sunday school time. This still leaves a person with a disability in a segregated situation.

7. Jean Vanier, *Community and Growth* (Mahwah: Paulist Press, 1979), 5.

8. Thomas Groome, *Christian Religious Education* (New York: Harper & Row, 1980), 126.

9. Janet Soskice, *Metaphor and Religious Language* (Oxford: Clarendon Press, 1985), 153–54.

10. Webb-Mitchell, *Christly Gestures*, 44.

11. Ibid., 44.

12. Ibid., 50.

13. Ibid., 43.

14. Webb-Mitchell, *Christly Gestures*, Part II.

15. John Howard Yoder, *Body Politics* (Nashville: Discipleship Resources, 1992, 51.

16. Ibid., 60.

17. Ibid., 51.

18. Brett Webb-Mitchell, "Living Into the Body of Christ: Toward Full Inclusion of People with Disabilities Into the Church," ACSWP Report, Presbyterian Church (USA) 2007.

19. Webb-Mitchell, *Christly Gestures*, 90.

20. Ibid., 90–91.

21. Dietrich Bonhoeffer, *Cost of Discipleship* (New York: Macmillan Press, 1975), 344.

22. Webb-Mitchell, *Christly Gestures* 170.

23. Martijn Pater, "Co-Creation's Five Guiding Principles," The White Paper is available through *Fronteer Strategy* (info@fronteerstrategy.com), April 2009. The principles are as follows: 1) inspire; 2) select; 3) connect; 4) share; 5) continue.

24. Ronald Rolheiser, *Holy Longing* (New York: Doubleday, 2000), 74.

25. Webb-Mitchell, 225.

26. Webb-Mitchell, 240.

27. Webb-Mitchell, 240.

CHAPTER EIGHT

Practicing Love

*Make no mistake about it, the secret to discovering thin places
is not in finding some coveted geographical location.
The secret is inside of us.*
—LONNI COLLINS PRATT AND DAN HOMAN[1]

To say that God is love is either the last straw or the ultimate truth.
—FREDERICK BUECHNER[2]

*Forgiveness is the beginning, the middle and the end of gospel life . . .
Forgiveness is the supreme work of God for the re-creation of all things.
Nothing new happens without it.* —RICHARD ROHR[3]

*But strive for the greater gifts.
And I will show you a still more excellent way.*
—1 CORINTHIANS 12:27

Thin Places, Holy Gatherings

The first chapter of this book was a brief survey of the various ways the community of people with disabilities and people in faith communities—many of whom were able-bodied—interacted or did not interact with one another. The survey began with a quick trace of how people with disabilities and their families were initially left to forage on their own. By and large, people with disabilities of all ages depended upon the good will of individuals and family members to care for them.

With the beginning of institutionalization, especially in the late nineteenth century, there was a wall, literally and figuratively, that separated people with disabilities from faith communities in particular, and the public in general. The wall that separated people with disabilities from people who are able-bodied was thick and high. At first, the hope was to give people living within the walls of an institution assurance that they were safe from harm and well protected. Later, it was people who were non-disabled who needed assurance that they were safe from people with disabilities who lived behind the walls of an institution. Sometimes these walls were actually concrete, stones stacked on stones, high shrubbery, or tall iron posts, and not always attractive to the eyes. Other times these walls were more figurative, made up of people, professionals and lay people alike, who kept people with disabilities and people who were non-disabled divided. Literally or figuratively, the wall was sometimes carefully tended to and bolstered through years of attention and skilled maintenance. But behind even the most beautiful wall there was hiding a thick, often angry, violent, and oppressive wall that separated people with disabilities and people who are non-disabled, whether in the Church or in society at large.

As documented here and in many other books, in recent decades the movement of deinstitutionalization in the 1960s and 1970s allowed more people with disabilities out of the institutions and into the neighborhood and public square, whether either the able-bodied public or people with disabilities were ready or not. Many people with disabilities who did not have families simply fell between the ropes or netting of the social welfare programs. Then, with the passage of the Americans with Disabilities Act in 1990 and additional legislation that paid for special education programs and provided equal access to housing, people with disabilities increasingly campaigned for their civil rights and "self determination." People with disabilities were no longer waiting for the rest of society to catch-up to the equal rights of *all* people, able and disabled alike. Today, largely because of the various social programs and movements, the wall of separation between people who are disabled and able-bodied is thinner, but not yet removed. There still exists a thin separation, a thin place, a semblance of segregation between people with disabilities and people who are non-disabled in society in general and the Church in particular. We still live in a "separate but equal" climate in this country.

The idea of thin places is a recurrent theme in and among those who visit sacred sites, often construed as a positive and powerful presence. For example, Lonni Collins Pratt and Dan Homan write that there are "sequestered, sacred spaces on earth where, if you listen very carefully, you can hear God more clearly and feel God more closely than you thought possible."[4] The spiritual assumption is that sometimes there is a thick, dense wall between us and God that makes us feel that we are all by ourselves. At such times, it feels like it's "us" (mortal creatures) versus "them" (the Holy Trinity). Other times it is as if there is no wall at all: "Should you press your hand against it, a hand presses back, and should you whisper to it, a Voice answers," write Pratt and Holman.[5] Sometimes that wall is outside of us in geographical or architectural places, and sometimes that wall is spiritual and within us, in which the secret of getting through it is to be discovered by us all as we seek full communion with the Holy One.

Likewise, such a thin wall, a thin place, within our own lives and between those who are able-bodied and disabled, makes it feel like we have walled ourselves off for all kinds of reasons from our families, friendships, colleagues, and sometimes with our selves. But for the purposes of this book, the spotlight is on breaking through this last vestige of a wall, thin as it is, between people with disabilities and people who are non-disabled. It is the intent of the author, in this book on inclusion, that we move through and finally remove the thin membrane, the thin impediment that separates and still divides us, whether that separation is in architecture or programs, in the gestures expressed or not expressed to one another, or the small cleft within relationships of the heart. It is my hope that we will one day move to a place, to a time, to relationships, when *all of us*, with all of our abilities and inabilities, limitations and gifts, may envision our oneness in Christ. This is made possible not by our works, but by the grace of God that saves *all of us*. With the Spirit's leading, we may one day realize rather than simply verbalize the truth that we, who are many "are one body in Christ, and individually we are members one of another" (Rom. 12:6). Infused with grace through faith, employing the practice of love through our close alliance, work, play, education, and advocacy relationship with each other, there is the possibility of moving beyond any separation between two groups of people into being one people in Christ Jesus.

In this closing chapter, I first want to address the other places where there has already been progress as we move closer to no longer referring to "those of *us* who are non-disabled" versus "*them*, you know, the ones who are disabled," or vice versa, but move to a collective "we," "us," and "our" in and as the body of Christ. A community of faith that practices such inclusivity is a place and a people who are already conscious of the practices of welcome, acceptance, and inclusion, regardless of what one can or cannot do, or who one is or is not in the circle of faith.

Special programs of "disability awareness training" or "Disability Sunday" created to raise consciousness are no longer needed because an inclusive congregation or parish is at a point in their collective life story where *all* have and know their place within the body of Christ. My hunch? The God who is within all of us, the Holy Spirit that dwells among us, is conducting a quiet revolution as we are finding ourselves more and more often in serendipitous moments of fellowship and in relationships with each other that would have been impossible only a few decades ago. Sadly, the examples I have collected below of co-creative inclusiveness do not come from the implementation of large programs or policies created by national boards of Churches. There are still plenty of faith communities—whether a church or an intentional community like l'Arche—where the language and thus the practice of segregation of people who are disabled from those who are able-bodied is propagated. As long as we use the language of "dis-abled" or "dis-eased" there will be segregation.[6] That is why the second and last part of this chapter highlights the importance of Christ-like love, which challenges faith communities in general, and those congregations and parishes that are part of the larger body of Christ in particular, to finally welcome one and all as part of the Creator's marvelous creation.

Stories of Thin Places:
Signs of Growing Inclusivity

Inclusivity in the Public Square

In my search for inclusive, co-creative faith communities, I find that there is little evidence of such co-creation among faith communities. I have participated in meetings with members of the World Council of Churches and National Council of Churches of Christ, and cannot identify a church or a denomination that is closer or closest to being fully inclusive.

As a result, I look around me for examples of co-creative inclusivity in places and people outside the walls of the Church in the public square. Some of these places and communities of people exist because we live in a world where people with disabilities are earning money, going to college, marrying or living in significant relationships, and participating in the public square debates.[7] I am reminded of how inclusive the place where I live is when I hear an electronic "chirping of birds" when a traffic light signs that it has turned green and it is safe to walk across the street for all of us, including a person living with a visual impairment. I stop at the elementary school baseball diamond on my way to lunch to watch a softball game played by people who are visually impaired but who can follow the flight of a ball by listening to the "pinging" sound it makes on a summer's day.

I see people using sign language unapologetically at other sporting events, whether or not anyone else knows what they are signing. Such freedom of expression is contagious. People in power chairs politely ask me to move over as they scoot by me on the sidewalks of Carrboro, North Carolina, and then turn around and tell me about a tree root that disrupts the even flow of the sidewalk, with the cautionary words, "Watch where you walk or you'll trip!" I tour art museums alongside people who are using oxygen tanks, and notice the Braille descriptions of the paintings, next to the Spanish and English descriptions. I gather together with friends for money-raising events for people who are living with HIV in "first" and "third world" countries, with no one caring about anyone's gender, sexual orientation, or hidden disease. And I work out at the local YMCA alongside a young man who is living with cerebral palsy who is getting more toned each day as he gets close to surpassing me in the weight he can bench press.

In other places, the right to vote is being brought to group homes of people who were once thought "un-able" or "dis-able" to vote. More restaurants and shops, places in the public square, have bathrooms that are retrofitted or being built with an "eye" toward being accessible to people with disabilities. It is commonplace to find curbs cut along city streets and sidewalks, making it easy for people to navigate their power chairs. The person who helps me with grocery shopping may be someone who lives in a transition home and is learning to live as someone in recovery. People who live with a condition that falls in the spectrum of autism or autistic behaviors are now attending college, getting jobs, dating, marrying, and divorcing, just like people who are non-disabled.

This list could easily be expanded.

The Bedouins of the Sinai Wilderness

Another unexpected place of inclusion was discovered on a recent pilgrimage in the Egyptian Sinai desert, where our gathering of pilgrims had the good fortune to spend one night with a group of Bedouins. One of the amazing interactions that occurred that evening happened with a group of six or seven Bedouins that had joined us around our campfire: one of the Bedouins was deaf. Deafness is a common occurrence among Bedouins because of in-breeding.

What caught my attention was the way that the other Bedouins communicated with him using sign language, with people freely interpreting and signing back and forth with no one missing a beat or a joke. The interchange was fluid and normal, and no one seemed to notice that there was anything unusual or different about someone with a hearing impairment among us. In asking Moussa, our pilgrim guide, about this interaction, which seemed as natural as the conversation among the hearing pilgrims, he simply said—with a matter-of-fact tone—that this is quite natural among the Bedouins. They all learn sign language at an early age in order to communicate with each other.

The beauty of the interaction was that no one was left out of the conversation because they could or could not hear. In coming back to the States and attending worship the following Sunday morning, I kept looking around for anyone in the congregation who was signing, finding no one. They do have someone interpreting worship in Spanish, but not American Sign Language. Yet I know there are people in my community who are deaf who would appreciate someone who could sign. What, I wondered, would it be like to be part of a faith community in which it was "natural" to learn sign language in order to communicate with one another without making much of a fuss about it?

Dancing without the Lights On

On a recent television show, I was intrigued about the power of taste that is heightened when diners are brought into a darkened room and are unable to see the food that is before them. The diners were amazed at how much more they enjoyed the food in the dark when compared to eating food in the light. This made me think of other senses that are heightened when the lights are down low, namely smell, movement, and touch.

I am reminded of the time I found myself on the dance floor at a wedding reception in Washington State. I performed the wedding of a former student with her new husband from England. They had both met when they were living and working in an alternative, intentional Christian community with people with disabilities in England. The dance floor was filled with family members from both sides of the

Atlantic, including some members of the community where the couple met. The dance space was alive as we moved to the popular music of the 1960s, 1970s, and 1980s. What was amazing was what happened when the lights were turned down low, so that it was almost pitch black. With no disco ball or strobe light to penetrate the dark, you couldn't tell who was dancing with whom. We were *all* dancers at a certain point, moving, jumping, swaying, clapping hands, and laughing as we rocked out to rock-and-roll music. It dawned on me as we danced that no one knew or cared about who was or who wasn't disabled. It simply did not matter at all. We were all dancers, each and every one of us. It was only when someone turned on the lights that we suddenly realized any differences among us, yet I still noticed that these differences did not matter at all. For here, in this context, we were all dancers of the dance of life!

Striving for "A More Excellent Way"

What is amazing in all of these stories are the ways that the boundary or the division between people with disabilities and people who are non-disabled diminished or were in the process of diminishing as we drew closer to inclusivity and inclusion. The thin membrane or wall was growing less distinct; the line blurred between "able-bodied" and "disabled" and the process of co-creative inclusion was nearer to being our shared reality.

In light of these examples of inclusive communities or gatherings of people, the last question for this book is this: how can we replicate the process of creating a space, a place, and a relationship in which people who are disabled and those who are able-bodied are all included in our faith communities? What can we do to learn how to worship, to be shaped and formed in the gestures of friendship in the school of the Church, and to be in fellowship and active in service with one another, right where we live? To say this in another way: how or what kinds of practices, be they rituals or less grand actions, must be enacted so that participants in our faith communities will develop or implement a way of being inclusive of *all* members of the body of Christ? In the larger society of which we are a part, legislation dictated actions in the public square that resulted in pushing and prodding our society to be more just and equitable with people with disabilities. Laws removed at least some of the obstacles that prevented people with disabilities from being equal participants in the public square. So what will it take for our faith communities to move to a place of equanimity among all since we do not have the power of law to mandate justice or inclusivity?

The answer: In faith, believing and acting as if we are the body of Christ, in which grace and love are central to our way of being in this world!

We must begin by reclaiming who and whose we are: we are the Church as the body of Christ. That is the context in which this book is written. And because the Church *is* the body of Christ, we are incapable of controlling or manufacturing or managing what may happen within it once people who simply desire to follow Jesus and be one of God's people get together—regardless of whether one is living with or without a disability. Writes Richard Rohr: "Grace comes when you stop being preoccupied and stop thinking that by your own meddling, managing, and manufacturing you can create it."[8]

In our everyday life, or in the life of our work and careers, we are taught to be managers, people who can finesse and massage schedules and expectations. This is not all that bad for many human-oriented products and projects. But what we are playing with here in the body of Christ is the Holy. Again, as Rohr reminds us: we cannot manage and maneuver and manipulate spiritual energy. It's a matter of letting go. It's a matter of getting the self out of the way, and becoming smaller, as John the Baptist said. It is a matter of being awake, of being aware, of moving with the flow of God's grace, God's Spirit, who is doing something new in bringing together two communities that have often been separated in something wholly and holy new, always being formed and re-formed in the image of the body of Christ, namely the Church. Once we bring together or are brought together—people who are disabled and people who are able-bodied—in the context of the body of Christ, and once we stop managing what will or will not happen and let the Spirit lead, then something amazing is bound to happen.[9]

In addition to reclaiming who and whose we are, inclusiveness also requires that we adhere to the "law" of love. In his book *Wishful Thinking*, Frederick Buechner writes that God's law, which is love, has been stated in eight words: "Whoever does not love abides in death. (1 John 3:14). Buechner writes "Like it or not, that's how it is . . . it is the law as the 'way things are.'"[10] Buechner argues that this is not a law of the way things ought or should be, but is the way things are for Christians. It is important to learn and re-learn the practice of love in the process of practicing co-creative inclusion in our faith communities.

While countless theologians and biblical scholars struggle with the triune definition and expression of love—whether *philial*, *eros*, or *agape* as expressions of love in the Christian worldview—it is with agape love, this self-giving love or charity that means that one is willing to lose oneself "in another's arms or in another's company, or in suffering for all who suffer, including the ones who inflict suffering upon us," that we discover that to lose ourselves is to find ourselves.[11] As most theologians and biblical scholars are quick to point out, love is not merely an emotion, but is itself a gift that is to be practiced. Agape or charitable love is what the Apostle Paul writes of and points to in describing the nature of the body of Christ. In 1 Corinthians 12:27, we read these last words: "But strive for the greater gifts. And I will show you a still more excellent way." Likewise, the author of the letter to the Ephesians writes: "But speaking the truth in love, we must grow up in every way into him who is the head, into Christ, from whom the whole body. . . . promotes the body's growth in building itself up in love" (Eph. 4:15, 16).

The "thing" that keeps us moving, that doesn't stop the flow of progress toward inclusivity within the body of Christ, is love. But it is not "my" love, or human love that is the motivator, but the love of the One who loved us into being in the first place, and desires a relationship to this very day, regardless of our actions or what we can or cannot do. Rohr is right in insisting that Christian life has little to do with whether I or someone else is doing anything right. "It has everything to do with falling in love with a Lover who does everything right."[12] The One who motivates us to do what we do out of love is the one who loved us first and always, namely God, the author of love. This Godly love is known and is to be practiced within these five moves: first, truly listening or understanding where another person is coming from in his or her own loneliness; second, forgiveness for all that has gone on in the past and present in order to prepare for a season of new hope; third, the undergirding of love; fourth, respect; and fifth: justice and love.

Love in Listening with the Heart

I do not mean to be getting sentimental or terribly emotional in this last chapter, but in our relationship with those we love, metaphorically speaking, do we listen to each other with our hearts, deep down inside to the core of our very being? After all that has been written in this book about hearing impairments and deaf culture, it is nevertheless important in the process of moving forward in being the body of Christ with one another to understand at least metaphorically or analogically the gift of hearing, of listening, or of being understood. Lonni Collins Pratt tells the story of a Benedictine monk—Br. Ben—who is, by and large, deaf. Br. Ben has learned to live with his disability while also living out the Rule of St. Benedict. He communicates with gestures of arms and hands when he is happy or when he is tired of a rebuilding project in his monastery.

At one awkward moment she writes of a time when they meet in the corridor of the monastery where he lives:

> He smiled, crushed me in arms made hard from a lifetime of cattle tending, and said, "Mass is early today." I nodded, then asked loudly, "How are you?" (He had been down with a cold.)
>
> He lifted his arms, making a great circle with them and drawing my attention to the ruins around him. His hands were raised palms up, in a kind of desperate petition. He rasped a distinctly old, Italian, male grunt of resignation. He wasn't happy with the changes happening in his home. That's how he was.
>
> I understood. "It must be difficult to have your home torn up this way," I replied.
>
> He nodded. He shrugged. Then Br. Ben took hold of my arm and said, "Let's go to Mass."[13]

What Lonni Collins Pratt recognizes in him is his ability to hear with the ear of the heart and be open with his feelings about what is going on in his home. She, in turn, learns to be in solidarity with and respects the solitude of Br. Ben.[14]

What I also appreciate about her story in regard to Br. Ben is that she does not try to belittle him or treat him as a child or someone "less than her." Instead, she is trying to be in solidarity *with him*, understanding his feelings and thoughts, sharing his pain and frustration with a sense of mutuality.

Love Is Forgiveness

In my early years of seminary and ministry, I would romanticize the Church as the body of Christ, a community of intense vulnerability, intimacy, and love. This image was in contrast to the image I grew up with that exists in many Presbyterian churches. I grew up in a corporate/CEO model of Church administration in many Presbyterian Churches, where the pastor is the CEO and the rest of the church is structured according to a corporate or business model.

In my work within the machinery or the structure of a major mainline denomination, I have witnessed the "sausage grinder" process that goes on as large institutions try to provide benefits for people within the Church. Sometimes there are abundant blessings and surprises as people's needs and wants are met. But there are times that the structure itself is riddled with the sin of injustice and oppression, even toward people with disabilities.

What people like Harriet McBryde Johnson and others in the disability rights, self-determination groups point at in the Church is the sense that faith communities have often, if sometimes unintentionally, wanted to do is add an additional and new crutch to a person who is learning to walk with little assistance, a new obstacle or a new hurdle for people with disabilities to contend with in order to be part of a faith community. I have heard some people with disabilities simply insist that "leaning on the everlasting arms of God" (to quote an old hymn[15]) or needing to lean on Jesus is to force a person with a disability who is just learning to live independently back into a forced and fixed dependent relationship.[16] As I advocated in chapter six, in worship with a strong theme of confession and justice there will need to be a time for reconciliation and forgiveness to be practiced openly and often in order to right the wrongs that have found their way in the systems that support churches and other communities of faith.

Love Is Establishing Genuine Friendships

In *Radical Grace*, Richard Rohr writes this about love:

> [L]ove is not a feeling or an infatuation. It is a decision to lay down your life. Unless you know that God has laid his life down for you, unless you know that she has surrendered herself for you, you cannot understand love as decision. Whenever you want to know how to love, or how not to love, simply ask the question: how does God love me? God's love is patient; it is not jealous; it endures; it does not take offense; it waits, believes, hopes, forgives (1 Cor. 13:4–8). That's the way we must learn how to love one another. Love is a practical decision to *act on what is*—and *for* what is.[17]

To live the body of Christ in our congregations and parishes as an inclusive body, we will need to decide to love at all costs, even with our very lives. Godly love is an audacious challenge to the average, the ordinary way of living life with walls of fear that are easily put in place, and can divide and separate us.

To act in Godly love is to go beyond opening doors widely and worshiping together once a week on a Sunday morning or evening, or midweek worship, or attending a random potluck meal or playing games in a youth group. It will mean engaging in mutually agreed upon, long-term friendships and not mere acquaintanceships or relationships. These friendships between people with disabilities and people who are seemingly non-disabled will need to be open about the beauty and challenges of life. If friendship is one place where we are schooled in the virtues of the Christian life, as argued and proposed by many theologians, then a fully mutual, life-sharing friendship between people with disabilities and people who are non-disabled is the only way forward.

Much will be called upon in such friendships. For example, what has yet to be explored more fully is the issue of intersecting identities as a person is more than her or his disabilities or abilities. We are also shaped by our gender, our sexual orientation, our wants, our needs, our desires, our dreams, our economic class, our educational background, our career, our family, our social and health service "war stories," and our age—to name a few of the identities that clamor for being the primary variable in our lives. This is where life gets interesting as we start to peel back the onion layers of our life stories with one another, getting good and vulnerable with one another, revealing the joys and the horrors of injustice often perpetrated upon people with disabilities because people with disabilities are considered easily marginalized. It is an intimacy which, if not dressed up, can unleash a great sadness but a kind of catharsis that comes only once in a great while. It can truly be a moment in which one resonates with the very resurrection-storied life of the living Christ.

But the benefits of sharing our life stories with one another is to realize that, first, we are not alone. Second, that such sharing is truly an act of love. And third, that with this act of love we have made a decision to live life fully, just as we are, with those who love us, even when they know all about us.

Love Is Respect

In listening, hearing, receiving, seeing, and sensing the storied lives of countless people whom the world calls disabled, and living now as an openly gay man who is also quickly marginalized and treated as a second-class citizen in society and the Church, there is one word, and one emotional, intellectual, and physical reaction that I hope you, dear reader, will understand. Those of us who are marginalized, who are set aside as Outsiders, who are living life now more fully than we ever thought possible, who are deciding to love by laying down our lives and letting you know our stories—as God would want—simply ask for one thing: respect. Do not merely tolerate the presence of people with disabilities in your midst. Instead, respect those who live life fully with a disability, with a limitation, with a constant awareness of what one is un-able and able to do, yet knowing who they are, and whose they are, which matters most. We are people, crafted, molded, and energized by the Holy Spirit, who are doing amazing things, going beyond expectations and beyond what we all thought or imaged possible . . . truly going beyond accessibility and into the fully inclusive community of Christ.

Love Is Justice Restored

In *Where Do We Go From Here: Chaos of Community,* Martin Luther King Jr. wrote that "Power, at its best, is love implementing the demands of justice. Justice at its best is love correcting everything that stands against love."[18]

Parts of this book have explored the role of love as the motivating force and glue that holds the body of Christ's members together, in all our brilliant diversity, contrary points of view, theological areas where we "agree to disagree," and enables us to live in the questions of faith as we await an answer or response. But love is also in pursuit of justice when love is blocked and kept away from certain segments within the body of Christ, let alone in the world.

In this book, there have been plenty of stories of people with disabilities who have felt "left out" and disconnected from the love of God in Christ, located in the very marrow of the body of Christ. But the Spirit's love will not be hampered or withheld from any segment, population, or group because of what a person can or cannot do. That is why people with disabilities, their families, friends, and advocates, seek justice: so that love will win out for all.

A Post-Disability Ministry Church

Even though I am guilty of dreaming of an "ideal" or "utopian" church shaped in large part by the reign of God breaking into our collective lives and consciousness, consider for a moment what a church might look, sound, smell, taste, and feel like in a day and age when special attention to people with disabilities and disability ministry is no longer needed or necessary:

- There would be no more "handicapped parking" designated spots in parking lots. Such markings would not be needed because people would be conscientious enough to leave those spaces available for those who need to park closer to the doors of a sanctuary or fellowship hall.

- There would no longer be the announcement during worship by a liturgist or pastor "if you are able" when the congregation rises for singing or prayer because it would be assumed that people would do what they could or could not do, and not every hymn or prayer necessitates people standing automatically, whether a person is able-bodied or disabled.

- There would be flexible seating instead of hard wooden pews in sanctuaries, along with moveable seating in fellowship and educational classrooms. Cutouts of pews would no longer be necessary.

- Worship would involve many ways of communicating and relating to each other, whether it is through music, art, mime, pottery, drama, dance, the spoken word, visual art, screens, or web design. All would learn the language of others who do not speak, read, or listen as many others do in educational, fellowship, worship, prayer, and service opportunities. Simply because a person does not speak, read, or listen does not mean that a person does not understand or know what is happening in his or her world. Leadership in worship is chosen or decided upon by the gifts that a person brings, rather than opting for worship being led by primarily those who are non-disabled.

- Allowances would be made for different transportation pathways around a church structure.

- Allowance of time and energy would be made for creating and participating in worship that is meaningful for all, regardless of what a person can or cannot do. As a Presbyterian minister, it has been stressed to me in my education and in my preaching that the core reason we were created was and is to worship God. And that means "all of us" were created to worship God.

- All people would be available to assist one another in living the Christian life by communicating with one another about the needs of individuals and the community. It does not matter if someone is "able-bodied" or "disabled"; all may be given an opportunity to serve one another in love.

- In this computer age, with all the resources that are available to us at the "click" or pressing of a button, there is no reason that all the materials that are published or produced could not be accessed for *all* members of a faith community, regardless of how they know and are known in this world.

- Leadership and participation in church governance, educational activities, youth programs, fellowship events, are open to all, made accessible to all, without remembering to include people with disabilities as an afterthought or "intentionally." It is simply, and naturally, assumed that those chosen to be part of any leadership role and function, as well as any and all activities within a parish or congregation, are those who have been called to lead and participate with little thought in the reality that we all bring our gifts and limitations to whatever activity we choose to participate in.

These are but starting discussion points of what could be in the not-too-distant future.

We, Who are Many, Are One Body in Christ

There are times in my life that a community has suddenly been created through a calamity of sorts, people drawn together because of some horrendous situation that occurred, in which a group of strangers simply rallied around one another and were instantly of one mind and body and spirit in how to deal with an issue at hand.

There are times on pilgrimage when I am by myself that I quickly find myself a part of a community of pilgrims, chatting and sharing life stories, posing the dilemmas of life, chewing on the problems of the world, where souls are bared to perfect strangers. And once the pilgrimage is over and the destination reached, the lines of community and communication are snipped and we return back to a place and sometimes a people where we are more strangers to ourselves than anyone else. We were vulnerable and thus intimate with others because we knew we would never see or hear from them again.

In this book, I end where I began, with the simple words of Paul echoing through the ages from a letter to a Church in Rome to communities of faith today and in the future. Paul's words were written with a sense of realism and authenticity. He did not point and write, "in the future, you will be one body in Christ." Instead, he stated what was so obvious for him but remains a promise for us: we *all* are united and connected unto Christ, through faith and by grace, and are in an inseparable relationship with one another as members of this body of incarnate love. No longer is anyone to call someone "able-bodied" or a "person with disability," but "brother" and "sister," members of the body of the risen Christ.

Notes

1. Lonni Collins Pratt and Dan Hollman, *Benedict's Way* (Chicago: Loyola Press, 2000), 230.

2. Frederick Buechner, *Wishful Thinking* (New York: Harper & Row, 1973), 54.

3. Richard Rohr, *Radical Grace* (Cincinnati: St. Anthony Press, 1995), 343.

4. Ibid., 229.

5. Ibid., 230.

6. I have already highlighted this issue in this book and other publications I've written and in the seminars and conferences in which I have participated, I agree that the issue of language is of high importance among people with disabilities, and thus should be for all of us. There were days when people with disabilities were considered "handicapped," referring to the begging gesture of putting one's cap in the hand and asking for alms. To this day, there are many publications that do not use "person-first" or "people-first" language whenever "people with" is placed in front of the disabling condition. Confusing the issue is that different "disabling conditions" are given names in other cultural contexts.

Whenever "disability" is used, or a disabling condition is expressed in written, signed, or spoken word, an "us" versus "them" context is created in which there cannot be equality or full inclusion. It is not until we move to a place, to a language, to a way of communicating with one another in which what a person can or cannot do is not highlighted or needed to be known or remarked upon, that we can be a community of co-creative inclusion, and thus true one-ness within the body of Christ.

7. Granted, there are churches of people who are deaf existing among some Protestant denominations, with little to no evidence of they're closing or going out of style soon. Being in a Church where people by and large use sign language is inclusive of people who are deaf or aurally impaired, but does nothing toward drawing a hearing and non-hearing congregation together. In a significant way, they are simply practicing what hearing congregations have done all these years: dictating that there will be one way of communicating and it will be with the use of one's aural sense. With no faith community that expresses itself in being co-creative and inclusive, I turn to the public square for small signs of inclusivity.

8. Richard Rohr, *Radical Grace*, 15.

9. Ibid., 16.

10. Frederick Buechner, *Wishful Thinking*, 50.

11. Ibid., 53.

12. Richard Rohr, *Radical Grace*, 23.

13. Lonni Collins Pratt and Dan Homan, *Benedict's Way*, 34.

14. Ibid.,35.

15. "Leaning on the Everlasting Arms of God," Words by Elisha Hoffman, Music by Anthony J. Showalter.

16. In Brett Webb-Mitchell, *Unexpected Guests at God's Banquet* (New York: Crossroad Pub. Co., 1994), there are many stories of people with disabilities whose primary gripe with the Church is that they were being forced to depend on Jesus just when they were in the process of gaining independence. Jesus became for many people a "crutch" to lean upon just as they were learning to walk on their own.

17. Richard Rohr, *Radical Grace*, 368.

18. Martin Luther King Jr., *Where Do We Go From Here: Chaos or Community?* (Boston: Beacon Press, 1968), 45.